Handwoven Home

WEAVING TECHNIQUES, TIPS, AND
PROJECTS FOR THE RIGID-HEDDLE LOOM

LIZ GIPSON

Published by Interweave Books, an imprint of F+W
Media, Inc., 10151 Carver Road, Suite 200, Blue Ash,
Ohio 45242. (800) 289-0963. First Edition.

fw

www.fwcommunity.com

21 20 19 18 17   5 4 3 2 1

Distributed in Canada by Fraser Direct
100 Armstrong Avenue
Georgetown, ON, Canada L7G 5S4
(905) 877-4411

Distributed in the U.K. and Europe by
F&W MEDIA INTERNATIONAL
Pynes Hill Court
Pynes Hill
Rydon Lane
Exeter
EX2 5AZ
United Kingdom
Tel: (+44) 1392 797680
E-mail: enquiries@fwmedia.com

SRN: 16WV01
ISBN-13:978-1-63250-338-1

EDITOR: Leslie T. O'Neill
TECHNICAL EDITOR: Susan Horton
COVER AND INTERIOR DESIGNER: Karla Baker
ILLUSTRATOR. Lee Ann Short
BEAUTY PHOTOGRAPHER: Dan Cronin
STEP BY STEP PHOTOGRAPHER: George Boe

CONTENTS

INTRODUCTION 4

PART ONE: WEAVING FOR THE HOME

CHAPTER ONE: Yarn for Interiors 6

CHAPTER TWO: Know-How for the Rigid-Heddle Weaver 18

CHAPTER THREE: Following the Patterns 30

PART TWO: PROJECTS

CHAPTER FOUR: The Kitchen 34

Four Looks Kitchen Towels 36

Fabric Stash Rag Rug 40

Light Bright Towels 46

Fresh Baked Bread Cloth 50

Linen & Lace Cafe Curtains 54

CHAPTER FIVE: The Dining Room 60

Hemp Hot Pads 62

Skip-a-Slot Placemats 66

Twill Be Done Runner 70

Four-Sided Fringe Napkins 76

Luxe Linen Placemats 80

Campy Gamp Runner 84

Go Your Own Way Runner 88

CHAPTER SIX: The Living Room 92

Hudson Bay Inspired Throw 94

Tweed and Twill Pillow Cover 98

Bejeweled Table Square 104

Oversized Mug Rugs 108

Mixed-Warp Pillow Cover 112

Mesaland Doubleweave Pillow 116

CHAPTER SEVEN: The Bathroom 122

Linen Facecloths 124

Bordering on Perfect Hand Towels 128

Two-Color Krokbragd Rug 132

PART THREE: BEGINNINGS AND ENDINGS

CHAPTER EIGHT: Warp Your Rigid-Heddle Loom 138

CHAPTER NINE: Finish Your Weaving 150

GLOSSARY 164

RESOURCES 166

INDEX 166

INTRODUCTION

I relish the quiet, contemplative moments in life—cooking a pot of soup, curling up on the couch with a good book, or taking the dog for a long walk. All of these activities are made better by textiles. Yes, even walking the dog is enhanced by textiles. It is on these walks that I work out my next weaving project. Weaving in your head counts!

Probably much like you, I look at curtains, floor coverings, table linens, and bathroom towels and think "How lovely would it be to weave that for myself!" I see a sunset, and I think "colorway;" I hike a high desert mesa, and I think "pattern."

On New Year's day 2015, I woke up with one of those lightning-bolt ideas. I had just moved into a new house, and it was a wide-open canvas begging for cloth. I decided I would weave something for every room in the house to realize a lifelong dream of living in a handwoven home.

My challenge was inspired by need. Next to the sink is a towel rack, which is handy because we have no dishwasher. We also have limited counter space, so the towels I had on hand were constantly competing with the other objects on the counter. Commercial towels were all too long.

As a weaver, I designed a fingertip towel in exactly the colors, materials, and size I wanted. Because I can weave multiple projects on one warp, I wove two fingertip towels and one longer and thicker towel to hang on the oven door. Made of a linen-cotton blend, these towels wear like iron—they will outlast almost all of their store-bought counterparts. They give me great pleasure every time I use them—and use them I do.

This is why we weave, even when we can buy towels for next to nothing at a big box store. Making our own is better. I can tailor the cloth to my needs—size, color, and texture—and make it of materials that last. I know the story of the yarn, and I remember all that happened in

What is a Rigid-Heddle Loom?

The rigid-heddle loom gets its name from the ingenious part of the loom called a rigid heddle. It is made up of two supports between which are held heddles—the plastic pieces with the eye in the middle. These heddles are spaced so that there are gaps between them. This construction makes up the clever slot and hole construction of the rigid-heddle loom.

The rigid heddle is used to evenly space the yarns, lift and lower the yarns threaded in the holes, and to press the yarn into place. These functions are all served by separate parts in the rigid-heddle loom's larger cousins, the floor and table looms. This simple construction is what makes the rigid-heddle loom so accessible to the beginner. Don't be fooled by its simplicity, though; with a little know-how you can weave virtually any cloth your heart desires.

my life as I wove it. Handwoven cloth is like a memory scrapbook that you can use.

Weaving is particularly suited for the home. Looms produce long rectangular objects perfect for efficiently and effectively making all your home textiles—rugs, pillows, throws, curtain, placemats, runners, and towels. I use the words "efficiently" and "effectively" purposefully. Once you have the loom set up—and the rigid-heddle loom is extremely easy to set up—producing multiples of a project is relatively simple.

Your projects come off the loom practically as finished objects that need only your finishing touch. How elaborate the finishing is up to you. Simple hemstitching requires no additional finishing, or you can enhance your textiles with elaborate knotting that no machine can do. Using two heddles, you can create pillows that only need to be seamed on one end or throws and tablecloths that are twice as wide as your loom.

In my previous book, *Weaving Made Easy*, I covered the fundamentals of weaving on a rigid-heddle loom for crafters who know next to nothing about weaving. If you are brand-new to this style of weaving, you may find that book helpful. While writing *Handwoven Home*, I assumed you have at least one project under your belt and are familiar with some basic terms. I have included abbreviated warping information in the back of the book so you don't have to search for that information elsewhere, particularly the more advanced setups of indirect and two-heddle warping. There is a lot of jargon in any craft, so if you are confused by some of terms, refer to the glossary in the back of this book.

The ability to create a textile for your specific purpose is one of the best reasons to weave. Having the skills and techniques to do so gives you the confidence to tackle any project your heart desires. It is my hope that this book, which is one part recipe book and one part technique manual, will serve as your guide for creating textiles that you can live with for a lifetime.

CHAPTER ONE

YARN for INTERIORS

Selecting yarns for home projects is different than selecting yarns for wearables. Keep in mind that table linens and towels are washed regularly, window treatments are exposed to sunlight on a daily basis, rugs are trod upon, and cushions are sat on.

Yarn is the base material from which a weaver's particular brand of fun is made. I am not a big fan of rules, but I am a huge fan of knowledge. If you know a bit about yarn, how it is made, what makes one yarn different from another, and how this relates to the projects you make for your home, you will have more fun at the loom and find even more happiness with the final product.

Yarn Content and Construction

The incredible world of yarn design is a marriage of fiber and construction. To make the best choices for your home décor projects, it pays to learn a bit about what goes into the making of yarn.

As a handspinner, I can wax poetic about yarn construction for ages, but I'll spare you and focus on what you need to know as a weaver.

RAW MATERIALS

The basic building block of yarn is fiber. Natural fibers—cotton, linen, hemp, silk, wool, mohair, and the like—all have different fiber lengths referred to as a staple length. Among other factors, the length of the fiber determines how much twist the fiber needs to have enough integrity to stay put during use. Short fibers such as cotton need a lot of twist. Long fibers such as silk and mohair need less twist.

Other factors go into manufacturing decisions such as the diameter of the individual fibers, the crimp or natural wave of the fiber, the luster or how the fiber refracts light, and the way the fiber was harvested. How the yarn is prepared and twisted will ultimately decide how these properties will be brought forth.

PLY

Also, you will hear the word "ply" thrown around a lot. An individual strand of fiber twisted together is called a singles or a single ply (ply here being a noun and not a verb). These singles can be used on their own or plied with other singles for a variety of reasons—to impart more strength, to make a thicker yarn, or to balance the yarn. Different fibers call for different treatments.

Tightly spun smooth yarns are traditionally thought of as good weaving yarns. Loosely plied or softly spun yarns are often shunned. There is a trade

Whether cotton, wool, or synthetic, tightly spun, smooth yarns are good for weaving.

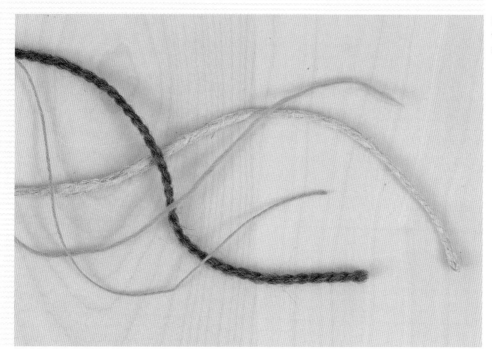

off between these two extremes. You want yarn that is strong, but you may also want it to be pliable, depending on your end use.

You may also run into the terms "woolen" and "worsted." From a yarn construction standpoint, they refer to the fiber preparation and spinning technique used to make the yarn. Worsted yarns are smooth, dense, long wearing, and create very good pattern definition. Woolen yarns are light, airy, fuzzy, and have more elasticity. To confuse matters evenmore, worsted is also a weight classification for knitting yarns.

YARN FOR THE RIGID-HEDDLE

The good news for the rigid-heddle weaver is that this loom allows you to use perhaps the widest range of yarns compared to other loom types. The rigid-heddle loom itself causes less abrasion and stress on the yarn than many other types of looms. Its relatively short distance from warp beam to cloth beam means you can get tight tension without a great deal of force.

Still, the weaver may be left wondering which yarn to use for which project and how do all the many cotton, wool, and other fiber-based yarns differ from one another. Knowing a little bit about yarn content and construction will allow you to make an informed selection when faced with a wall of yarn and a project you want to make.

Cellulose Fibers

For kitchen, dining, and bath projects, cellulose is king. Cotton, linen, and hemp yarns wash, wear, and weave beautifully. You won't find wool yarns in my patterns for the kitchen, dining room, or bath.

COTTON

Cotton is nature's way of protecting the seeds of the cotton plant until they are ready to germinate. It is a marvelous fiber; strong, cool to the touch, absorbent, non static, and resistant to abrasion. It requires a lot of twist for the yarn to have enough integrity to hold up to weaving's rigors.

I've noticed that if a pattern calls for cotton yarn, many weavers dig into their stash and pull out whatever cotton they have on hand. Conversely, some weavers are baffled by the wide variety of cottons and want to know which one to use for which project. All cotton yarns are not the same. Depending on their type, they will behave differently in the finished cloth.

MERCERIZED COTTON (aka perle or pearl cotton) is soaked in a sodium hydroxide bath. This increases the surface area of the yarn and gives it a shiny appearance. Mercerization increases the fiber's

In the kitchen, bath, and dining room, cellulose-based yarn is the go-to choice for weaving.

ability to take dye and strengthens it. It also slightly decreases the yarn's ability to absorb water. Mercerized cotton is the go-to for most household linens, such as table runners, placemats, pillows, and curtains. Strong as an ox, it can take whatever abuse you throw its way. It can work for towels, but I prefer unmercerized cotton's absorbency and it's relatively faster drying time.

UNMERCERIZED COTTON is just that, cotton that hasn't been mercerized. It has a nubby appearance that imparts a handspun look to the finished fabric, and it is highly absorbent. It isn't as strong as mercerized cotton.

COTTON CARPET WARP is a tightly twisted 4-ply unmercerized cotton. It is extremely strong and comes in a variety of colors. The hard twist makes it very stable and decreases its tendency to bloom or puff out in the wash. It is great as a base for rugs or mats, but if you use this yarn for a towel, it may have a stiffer hand than you may like.

ORGANIC COTTON is grown so that it retains much of the plant's natural wax in addition to avoiding the use

of petrochemicals for its production. This gives the yarn a lovely, buttery feel. In its unmercerized form, it is shinier than you might expect. It is a great choice for soft, absorbent towels.

NATURALLY-COLORED COTTON is grown in a range of natural colors from rich browns to lovely greens and reds, and it is also a great choice for towels. The industrial revolution and its need for uniformity almost drove these plants to extinction. Farmer and inventor Sally Fox rescued them and created a strain appropriate for mill spinning. You can't always judge its color by what you see on the cone, spool, or skein. This cotton often deepens when washed, producing richer, more intense hues.

CROCHET COTTON is easy to find in big box craft stores. It is designed for crocheters and is often used by tatters for its unique construction. Crochet cotton is mercerized and very tightly spun, opposite to most conventional yarns—spun to the left and plied to the right. The twist and ply direction don't really make a difference to weavers. Similar to carpet warp, it doesn't bloom as much as other cottons. It is a good substitution for Pearl cotton; just keep in mind that due to the extremely tight twist, it will be a bit stiffer and crisper looking in the final cloth.

CRAFT COTTON is my catchall name for a 4-ply, unmercerized yarn with moderate twist. It tends toward the light-worsted weight. Depending on the quality of the cotton, it can be an excellent choice for absorbent soft towels and other household items. However, it can be linty, depending on how tightly the yarn is spun. Cotton spun with low twist feels soft, but those short fibers tend to work their way out over time, causing your fabric to pill. These yarns may not create heirloom-quality fabrics, but they will hold up quite well to daily use.

RECYCLED COTTON is highly variable and fun to work with. It is made from the remnants of garment manufacturing. The waste is sorted in color lots, shredded, and remade into a lovely tweedy yarn that has a lot of character. This yarn can be used in a wide variety of projects, but don't fall in love with a particular colorway, because they can come and go from a yarn line pretty quickly.

NOVELTY COTTON is a pretty broad category. These yarns are softly spun, textured, and have a larger than expected grist for cotton. They can be used to create a lively textured fabric perfect for light-weight, decorative household items. They aren't a great choice for fabrics that are rubbed and wetted continuously, such as towels. These yarns will pill and shred with vigorous use. (Shaft-loom weavers avoid using them as warp because the metal or nylon heddles and reed will rip them to shreds, but rigid-heddle weavers can have at it!)

Some novelty cottons are finer and more tightly spun. Use the abrasion test to determine if they will work for you. I used a novelty cotton in the Go Your Own Way Runner as an accent yarn.

BAST FIBERS

Bast fibers such as linen, hemp, and jute have long been prized for the home. They wear well and have a unique drape and a crisp hand. Highly absorbent and

My Yarn Pantry

In the vast jungle of yarn possibilities, these are the yarns I go to over and over and over again for my home projects. I always have these five yarns at the ready, because I can make anything I want for my home from them:

- 22/2 cottolin*
- 8/2 unmercerized cotton
- 3/2 pearl cotton
- Worsted or DK weight wool
- Worsted-weight cotton or cottolin

This is about the the same size as an 8/2 cotton, but it is measured on a different count system; see "The Count System" section for more information.

Bast fibers such as linen and hemp make lovely, heirloom-quality fabrics that will last a lifetime.

cool to the touch, bast fibers are extremely durable, and their luster makes them ideal for heirloom-quality table linens and sophisticated curtains.

Bast-based yarns are extremely inelastic and like to be woven under tight tension. They transform during wet finishing as the fibers relax and move into position. A good pressing will also bring out their shine.

LINEN, the most common bast fiber, is made from the flax plant. Considered a luxury fiber, it is renowned for its use in fine home textiles.

HEMP is not all hype. It is a lovely fiber that is making a strong comeback. It is molecularly different from linen, so it takes dye better. It also resists mildew, which comes in handy for cloth used in wet environments, such as the bathroom.

JUTE is not often found in a very refined state. It makes an excellent rope that is good for use in rugs that receive a lot of foot traffic. Look for jute that is smooth and doesn't shed when you rub it.

COTTOLIN is a blend of cotton and linen. It adds a bit of elasticity to the linen, making it easier to work with, and the linen adds strength to the cotton. With repeated washings, cottonlin textiles sometimes

release a bit of lint. This is caused by the short cotton fibers working their way free of the long linen fibers.

Wool Yarns

Wool and other protein fibers deserve as much consideration for interior weaving projects as cotton. It struts its stuff in rooms meant for relaxing. If you are a fan of breed-specific wools on the long and strong side, interiors are the perfect application. (Check out the Tweed and Twill Floor Pillow.) Short, soft fibers such as Merino are lovely for next-to-skin wear, but they won't hold up well underfoot; if used in a pillow, they may pill with repeated use.

Longwools include breeds such as Border Leicester, Coopworth, Cotswold, Leicester Longwool, Lincoln, and Romney. Long, lustrous, strong, with wavy crimp, they are prized for their strength and high gloss. They don't felt easily and keep their shape wash after wash. Longwools result in smooth, sleek, worsted low-twist yarn that is strong. These yarns make great choices for rugs, pillows, and throws. Wool cloth comes to life when wet finished. During washing, wool yarns expand and settle in a process called "blooming."

THE PRICKLE FACTOR

Yarn folks tend to shy away from strong wools because they prickle, which is caused when the microscopic ends of the fiber work their way free of the yarn and give you a little poke. The thicker the diameter of the fiber, the stronger the poke. Although you may feel an initial sensation, it may dissipate quite rapidly as you relax into the textile.. I enjoy the long-wearing benefits and the pleasure of using long and medium wools, so I can live with a little poke.

Superwash Yarns

Superwash yarns are designed to be stable and don't bloom much. This is fine with the loopy construction of knitting and crochet, but it can be problematic in woven fabric. I use them only in fabrics that I want to be stable, such as the Oversized Mug Rugs.

Synthetic Fibers

Synthetic yarns are a vast class of yarns created in a lab, similar to superwash and mercerized yarns. Like all yarns, synthetics must be used appropriately. They tend not to be absorbent, so they are not good for towels; that lack of absorbency, though, can be great for table runners.

Synthetics also tend to be dyed in their raw state before put into yarn form, so the colors are through and through—not just on the surface of the yarn—making them more lightfast. This makes them a good choice for curtains.

Perhaps surprisingly, ynthetic yarns have a base of natural materials. Some are renewable, such as wood, bamboo, and soy; some are not, such as coal and petroleum. Although the fiber is created in a lab, when it heads to the mill, the same principles of fiber length, twist, and ply are used to create the final product.

RAYON, OR ARTIFICIAL SILK, are considered a semi-senthetic yarn and comes under all sorts of brand names such as Tencel and Soysilk. These yarns have either a cellulose base, such as wood or bamboo, or a protein base, such as soy or milk.

The base is cooked into a "batter," then fibers are extruded into a wide variety of yarns. They can be long, sleek, and shiny like silk, or lofty and airy like wool. They play well with other fibers and blends, and they make great curtain or pillow-cover fabrics. These yarns can be good alternatives for those who are allergic to wool.

NYLON YARN is derived from coal. It is shiny, tough, stretchable, and melts under a hot iron. The fibers are nonabsorbent, quick drying, and won't wrinkle. Nylon is often blended with other fibers to increase a yarn's toughness.

ACRYLIC YARN is petroleum based. The yarn is lightweight, warm, and quick drying. It has less stretch than nylon and can cause the same issues in cloth as superwash. Both types of yarn are designed to be stable and don't bloom in the final wash. Like nylon, blending acrylic with other fibers can lend both of their good qualities to the final yarn. Both of these yarns are inexpensive and designed for lots of wash and wear, but neither is very absorbent and won't make a good choice for kitchen and bath items.

NOTE: *All yarn production consumes resources—water, land, fuel, and labor. Most involve some sort of chemical. Just because a yarn is synthetic doesn't mean it's bad, and a yarn that is natural isn't necessarily good. Modern farming practices can be highly water intensive and use vast amounts of pesticides to create natural fibers. Some manufactured yarns use naturally growing renewable resources and less water than some of the natural counterparts—and some do not. Get to know your fiber and yarn to make the best choice for your home and lifestyle.*

Weaving vs Knitting Yarns

Industrially speaking, yarns that are manufactured for weaving and those manufactured for knitting are different. Weaving yarns often, but not always, have more twist. Some manufacturers leave in the spinning oil that protects the yarn from the rigors of the loom. This oil washes out when the fabric is finished, and the yarn transforms once released from the bounds of the oil.

This matters if you purchase mill ends, which are getting harder and harder to find; and if you find the perfect yarn, you may not be able to find that exact yarn again. As the name implies, these are remnants from commercial-weaving mills. If a mill-end wool feels rough to the touch, wash a little sample and see what happens. It may finish with a very different hand than what you find on the cone.

In recent years, as knitting has become more popular and consumer demand has increased, many manufacturers catering to the handcraft market changed their formulas. They have softened the yarn by decreasing the singles and ply twist and using more and more superfine and superwash wools.

Almost any yarn—made for weaving, knitting, or crocheting—can be used for weft. Still, consider how well it will wear over time and under the rigors of daily household use.

Yarn Put-Up

Yarns are sold in all sorts of ways, the most common being hanks, skeins, and cones. Traditionally, yarns for weaving were put up on cones because it was easier to wind a warp from the cone, and the fine cellulose and linen yarns popular with weavers get tangled when wound into skeins or hanks.

These terms have been somewhat muddied over the years. You may also hear a hank referred to as a skein. This is a technical definition used in some measurement systems that indicates a smaller unit size than a hank. This distinction has lost some of its meaning to the consumer. A skein is more commonly recognized as an oblong ball.

The Count System

New weavers often ask, "What is the deal with coned yarns and those funny numbers?" The numbers, such as 8/2 or 5/2, are part of the names of the fibers. This naming convention is called the Count System, a very old system established when each fiber, including wool, cotton, linen, and silk, had a separate industry-trade group responsible for setting the standards on yarn sizes.

Today, it seems a little nonsensical. A good manufacturer will provide the yards per pound and a balanced plain weave sett of the yarn, so you don't have to memorize what these numbers mean; but, it is helpful to know.

The first number is the relative weight of the yarn. The higher that number, the finer the yarn. So, a 5/2 yarn is thinner than a 3/2 yarn. The second number

The most common yarn put-ups are cones, skeins, and hanks.

is the number of plies in the yarn. So, a 5/2 yarn has two plies.

The cotton guild long ago determined that their system would be based on a skein of yarn that is 840 yards (768 meters). This base yarn would be a size 1/1, a singles yarn measuring 840 yards (768 meters)/lb. A size 2 yarn would require two skeins of thinner yarn to equal one pound or two skeins of even thinner yarn plied. So, a 5/2 yarn is a 2-ply yarn that measures 2,100 yards (1,829 meters) per pound; this is 840 multiplied by 5 and then divided by 2.

Choosing Warp and Weft Yarn

Whatever yarn you select, it must be able to hold up to the rigors of the loom as well as the wear and tear of daily use. Luckily, the rigid-heddle loom is an extremely yarn-friendly loom.

Weaving puts tension on the yarns collectively, not on each individual yarn. While you have to evaluate the yarn individually, you also have to understand how pressure is exerted on it within the framework of the loom.

The plastic heddles that make up the rigid heddle itself are gentler on yarn compared to other heddle types. The relatively short length of warp held taut between the beams allows you to use less tension than on a larger loom, which requires much more tension on the warp to prevent sagging in the middle. With this in mind, your yarn doesn't have to hold up to industrial standards. It just has to pass the simple pinch-and-pull test.

PINCH-AND-PULL TEST

To determine if your yarn is strong enough as warp, with the yarns held taut on the loom, give it the simple pinch-and-pull test: Pinch both ends of a 4"–6" (10 – 15 cm) section of yarn between your index finger and thumb. Apply steady, firm pressure as if to pull the yarn apart. If the yarn easily drifts apart or breaks, it will fail as a warp yarn.

If your yarn passes the pinch-and-pull test, observe the yarn with tension and without. Holding

The Count System
BASE NUMBERS

COTTOLIN: 300 yards
COTTON: 840 yards
WOOLEN (WOOL): 256 yards
WORSTED (WOOL): 560 yards
SILK: 840 yards
LINEN: 300 yards

* Woolen yarns are less compact than worsted yarns, so they have a lower count number in the Count System.

the yarn between your index finger and thumb again, observe it both under tension and in its natural state as you tug and release. Note how much elasticity the yarn has. Does it stretch and rebound? Or does it hold steady? This knowledge will come in handy when you are deciding how to use the yarn. If the yarn holds steady, then it should hold up to the rigors of the loom.

ABRASION TEST

Understanding how your yarn will wear can also be evaluated up front. Take a piece of yarn and rub it back and forth on the corner of a table vigorously a number of times. This is a good test of the yarn's ability to resist abrasion. If the yarn shreds or pills, it is most likely going to do this in your finished cloth.

Weft yarns, the yarns you weave with, don't have to pass the pinch-and-pull test. But if the yarn shreds or pills easily during the abrasion test, it may not be the best choice for home décor projects.

Fringes can be short or long, knotted or loose, or trimmed close to the work and encased in a hem.

Fringe Treatment

A final major consideration when selecting yarns for weaving is how they will act in the fringe. Singles yarns puff out in the wash, making little tufts. Plied yarns and some fancy novelties can fray. These can be negatives or positives depending on the look you are going for.

To get an idea of how the yarn will act in the fringe, cut a few pieces about 12" (30 cm) long and hand wash them vigorously in hot water with a little soap. Pay attention to how the ends behave—this will show you what will happen in the fringe.

Regardless of your tests, remember: All yarn will fray eventually. If you like the look of straight fringe,

handwashing is recommended. You can trim away ends that stray over time, and the fringe still shows off the yarn's beauty.

If your yarn has the potential to fray at the ends, finish them off with twisted or braided fringes and trim them close to the knots. You can trim away ends that stray over time, and the fringe still shows off the yarn's beauty.

Learning which yarn works best for what type of project comes with experience. The good news is that there are a wealth of projects in this book where I have done all that choosing for you, allowing you to gain experience as you make beautiful fabrics for your home.

CHAPTER TWO

KNOW-HOW
for the
RIGID-HEDDLE
WEAVER

Handweaving great cloth is like baking a cake. It is one part ingredients, one part know-how, and one part finishing touches. Selecting the right ingredients—yarn—understanding the right technique for the job at hand—know-how—and then adding your own personal details—finishing touches—is what makes a good cloth great. This chapter is all about the middle part, the know-how.

Go-To Tips and Techniques

When weaving for the home, I use a handful of techniques and tools over and over again. With this know-how, I can weave multiple projects that are all the same size, place design elements so they fall in the same place on each successive textile, make seamless transitions between colors, and create hard-wearing textiles. Perhaps most importantly, they allow me to head off potential problems before they become problems.

Following is a laundry list of go-to techniques that will help you weave with less fuss and more fun.

Weaving a Header

In almost every instance, I recommend weaving a header of smooth scrap yarn before you start to weave your project. A header is scrap yarn that is woven into the beginning and end of a project and removed later. The purpose of a beginning header is to spread the warp evenly so there are no gaps in the warp and to give your cloth a firm foundation on which to grow. I like to use a smooth cotton scrap yarn that contrasts well with the actual project yarns, making it easier to distinguish from my project yarns when I am ready to remove it.

You may be tempted to skip this step. But, unlike floor or table looms, the rigid heddle isn't secured to the loom. It hangs freely when you release it from the heddle block. You guide the rigid heddle toward the edge of your cloth to place the next weft with your hands. I recommend using both hands to guide the heddle into place. Even so, one side of the heddle always hits the cloth before the other. Typically, the side of your non-dominant hand will hit first because you have less control over it.

If you don't weave a header, you may notice that one side of your cloth grows faster than the other, causing your weaving to have a slight angle. This isn't the only reason this happens, but it is one of the most common reasons.

This may or may not cause issues in the final cloth. If you are weaving with wool, these irregularities will most likely fill in after you wash your project. However, if you are weaving with a yarn that doesn't bloom much, such as linen and tightly twisted cotton, these uneven lines may be more obvious. Also, fine threads tend to show irregularities more than thicker ones.

There is also the issue of finishing. If you are hemstitching, having the yarn spread evenly will ensure that your stitches are even. If you are knotting the fringe, the header will keep your weft in place until you are ready to finish, particularly when working with smooth, fine, or slippery yarns.

If you are knotting your fringe, you may also want to weave a footer with the same scrap yarn at the end of your project to keep the weft in place as you remove the fabric from the loom.

Managing Selvedges

Maintaining straight selvedges is the number two pain point for weavers, second only to warping tips. You must do the following three things if you want to maintain tidy edges and prevent draw-in:

WEFT ANGLE

The weft yarn doesn't travel in a straight line from selvedge to selvedge. It bends over and under the warp yarns. To allow enough length for the weft to do its thing, you need to lay it in at an angle before pressing it into place. How much of an angle depends on the width of the fabric and structure.

Your angle is too low if your selvedge begins to draw in, crowding the other threads. The angle is too steep if loops appear at the edges.

Experiment a bit before starting each project to determine the correct weft angle and then maintain that angle as you weave (photos 1 and 2).

ADVANCE OFTEN

Advance the warp after weaving 2"- 3" (5–7.5 cm) of cloth. The closer the cloth is to the rigid heddle, the greater the tension placed on the selvedge threads.

Another factor is that as your fabric grows closer to the heddle it becomes more difficult to maintain an appropriate weft angle.

WEIGHT YOUR SELVEDGES

Weighting your selvedges gives them an extra bit of tension, making it easier to maintain crisp edges. My favorite way to do this is to slip a 3" (7.5 cm) S-hook around each selvedge and let it hang off the back beam.

SLOT OR HOLE?

Yarns are threaded through a rigid heddle, alternating between slots and holes. Threading selvedges in a hole will result in a tighter tension at the selvedges than threading them in a slot. This may lead you to conclude that it would be best to have your selvedges in a hole, but I actually prefer them in a slot.

The slot yarns act more like a floating selvedge on a floor loom where the yarns aren't fixed in a heddle. Weighting them adds more tension and still allows you to manipulate them if necessary, such as when you're weaving certain pick-up patterns. However, not all patterns call for an odd number of warp ends, and some may require that you end in a slot on one side and a hole in the other side or a hole on both sides.

Weave a beginning header with scrap yarn to spread the warp evenly.

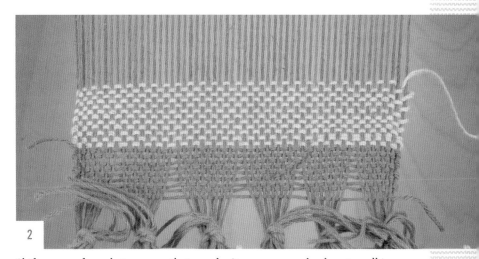

Shift your weft angle to ensure that you don't cause your selvedges to pull in or create extra loops at the selvedges.

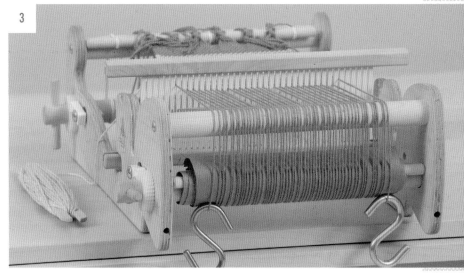

Weighting your selvedges adds extra tension and can help keep your edges tidy.

Using a Temple

Despite following the best practices for managing your selvedges, some patterns have a tendency to draw in more than others, particularly twill or weft-faced weaves. A temple is a handy tool to have to keep the weaving width even.

A temple is a stretcher with prongs or clips that pulls or pushes your weaving to a consistent width (photo 4). The most common temple is made of wood or metal and adjusts to multiple lengths. It has small sharp teeth on either side of the temple that allow you to place it at the edge of the fabric and then lock it in place at a fixed width.

When using a temple, you need to advance often, moving the temple up as you weave so that you always maintain the fixed width.

Managing Multiples

One of the best things about being a weaver is that you can put on a long warp and weave several towels, placemats, or napkins at one time. You can alter the color and pattern of each, making them unique, but coordinated. The challenge is weaving them all the same size, and if you have an accent—such as a stripe of pattern along the border, as in the Bordering on Perfect Towels—placing that pattern in the same place on every object.

MAKE A PAPER GUIDE

This is a trick handed from weaver to weaver. To ensure that your towels, for example, are all the same size and have stripes in the same place, make a thin paper guide and pin it to your warp as you weave.

Use a 3" (7.5 cm) wide strip of craft paper cut from a roll so that it already has a curl (photo 5). Cut it a bit longer than you want each of your multiples to be. Measure and mark the beginning and any hem or pattern marks along the way.

Roll the paper tightly from the end of the marking to the beginning and secure with a paperclip. Allow a 3" (7.5 cm) tab to stick out from the beginning of the project. Weave the first few inches (or several centimeters) of your project, then pin the guide to your work with a T-pin.

As you weave, roll out and re-pin the paper to your fabric. Use it as a guide to begin and end design elements and start and finish each weaving. When you finish one object, leave an appropriate amount of warp and start your next weaving, pinning and rolling the guide as you work.

Using a guide is a great way to measure your textiles as you weave. If you aren't weaving multiples, you can still use the same principle and pin a cloth tape measure to your fabric as you weave.

Measuring the Cloth

I often get the question, "Should I measure while the cloth is under tension or not?" Measuring under tension makes little difference with cellulose fibers such as cotton and linen, but it can make a big difference with yarns that have more elasticity. I recommend measuring wools and similar yarns with the tension backed off enough to allow the yarn to relax, but with enough tension so that you can measure it on a flat plane.

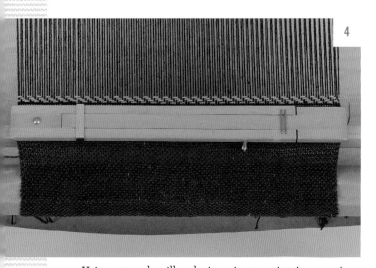

4

Using a temple will make it easier to maintain a consistent width while weaving.

Using a Tapestry Beater

A number of weft-faced fabrics in this book require the use of a beater, including the Skip-A-Slot Placemats, Oversized Mug Rugs, and Fabric Stash Rag Rug, just to name a few.

The rigid heddle isn't heavy enough nor does it have enough inertia compared to the weight of a beater on a floor loom to pack these textiles firmly enough. Using a tapestry beater to further pack the weft will give your fabric a firm, functional hand.

There are many styles of tapestry beaters. For most of the projects in this book, I recommend a 2" (5 cm) beater with prongs spaced ¼" (6 mm) apart with a wide base of at least 2" (5 cm) and a comfortable handle.

To pack the weft, stop every 1" (2.5 cm) or so and place the heddle in the position for the next pick—if you just wove an up shed, place the heddle in the down position or vice versa. This will lock in your weft threads. Then when you pack the weft, the threads will not be able to spring back in the same way as they would if the shed was open.

Use the tapestry beater to firmly pack the weft by starting in the middle of the weaving and firmly working out toward one selvedge. Then return to the middle and firmly pack the other side.

This will dramatically change the look of most patterns. You may not see the effect of the final pattern until you compact the weft.

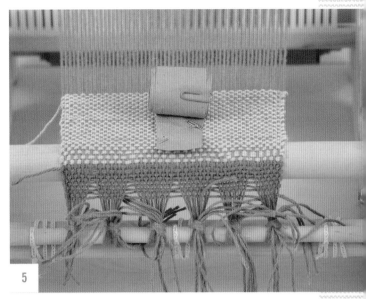

5

A paper guide can help make sure each project in a set of multiples is the same size and the patterns remain consistent.

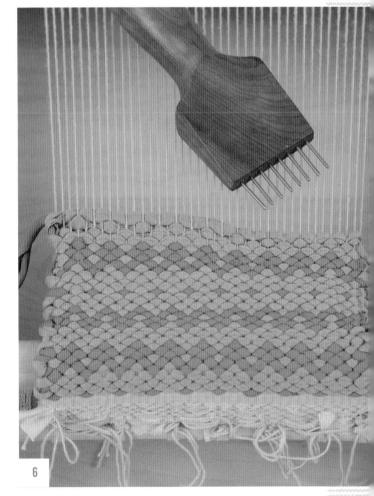

6

Using a tapestry beater will give your weft-faced weaves a firm, functional hand.

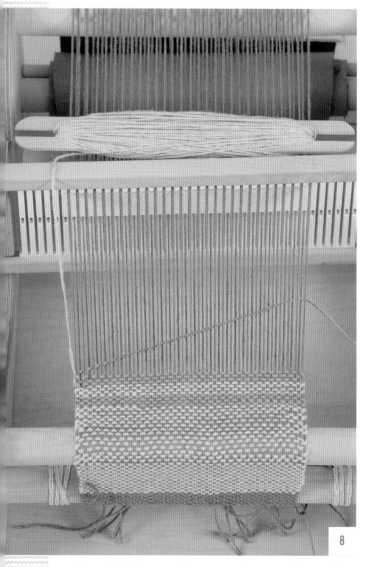

The tail-tuck method is the most common technique used to transition between colors.

For quick color transitions, carry the nonworking weft along the selvedge.

7

8

Changing Wefts

You can choose from a number of techniques to transition between one color or yarn to the next.

TUCKING TAILS

The simplest way to change weft colors is the good old tail-tuck method (photo 7). Cut the working weft, leaving a 6" (15 cm) tail, change the shed, and tuck the old color weft into this shed. Lay in the new color in this same shed, starting on the opposite side of the old color tail tuck, leaving a 6" (15 cm) tail. Press this pick and the old color's tail into place and then change sheds. Tuck in the new color's tail into the next shed and pass the shuttle through this same shed and press into place. This placement will put the tail tucks on either side of the weaving and decrease bulk.

However, if you are making multiple changes in quick succession, these joins can start to show or even cause your fabric to build up at the selvedges where the tails are tucked.

TRAVELING WEFT

When weaving with two colors that change frequently, leave the nonworking yarn active and interlock the working and nonworking wefts at the selvedge to diminish large loops. Treat the nonworking weft as you would the selvedge. If the selvedge is down, pass the working weft over the nonworking weft. If the selvedge end is up, pass the working weft under the nonworking weft.

Place the shuttle with the nonworking weft behind the rigid heddle, allowing it to follow the path of the selvedge thread. In this case, the last warp end (selvedge) is up, so the nonworking weft is also up. When you weave the next pick, pass the working weft under the nonworking weft.

PLY SPLITTING

When working with more than two colors that change frequently or with thick yarns, use the ply-splitting method to transition between colors. It creates an almost seamless join with little extra bulk. Ply splitting involves dividing the new and old weft tails in two equal sections. This is easy to do if you are working with doubled wefts, yarns with multiple plies, or even rags, which you can cut.

JOINING THE SAME COLOR

To join yarns of the same color, work the join in the middle of the cloth. Cut the yarn from the shuttle 6" (15 cm) longer than half the width of your cloth, and then split the weft in two for 6" (15 cm).

Place the heddle in the next shed, maintain your weft angle, and lay the weft into the shed, bringing it to the middle of the cloth. Pull out half of the split ply 4" (10 cm) from the end of the yarn and allow the other half to travel another 4" (10 cm), exiting it so a 2" (5 cm) tail sticks out from the shed.

Wind a new shuttle and split the end 6" (15 cm). Place the new weft in the same shed starting from the same side as the old weft. Pull the tail halfway through, stopping when the base of the split yarn is a few warp ends away from where the old yarn exits the shed. Place one half of the new weft in the shed and exit it after traveling 4" (10 cm), a few warp ends beyond the longer of the two old weft tails.

Press the yarn into place. Leave the tails in place until after washing the project, then trim them flush with the cloth.

TRANSITIONING TO A NEW COLOR

To start a new color, work a ply split of the old color at the selvedge. Then work another join on the opposite selvedge with the new color. Lay in the working weft as you would lay in a new pick. Cut the yarn from the shuttle, leaving a 6" (15 cm) tail. Pull the weft from the shed 2" (5 cm) from the selvedge. Lay one half of the ply back in the shed, wrap it around the selvedge, and place it back in the same shed, exiting it a few

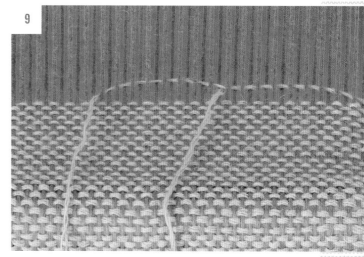

9

Ply Splitting: First, split the second yarn's tail and lay half of it in the same shed as the first yarn.

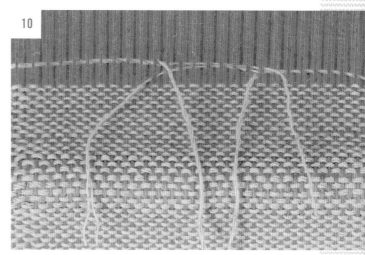

10

Then, split the first yarn's tail and lay half of it in the open shed.

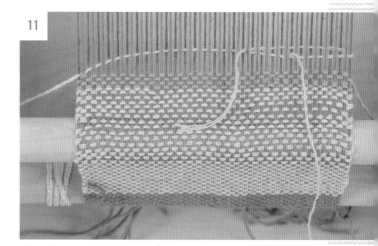

11

Ply splitting creates a virtually invisible transition between two colors and prevents build up at the selvedges.

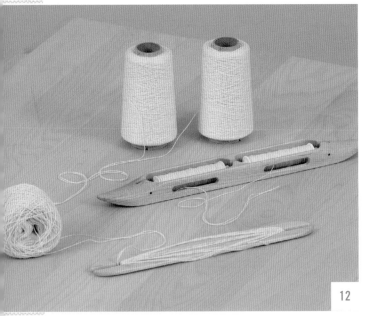

12

Wind doubled ends by using double-bobbin boat shuttles, winding from two separate yarn sources, or pulling from the outer and inner ends of a center-pull ball.

Doubling Ends

Doubling fine yarns and using them as one thread in the heddle is a great way to create fine cloth without using two heddles. The cloth will be a bit stiffer than if you used the yarn singly; however, depending on your use, this may not have an impact on its function. If you prefer the direct warping method, you can thread the holes at the same time you thread the slots, making it much easier to warp complex color orders. Do this warp as you normally would, but, instead of passing the yarn just through the slots, thread the holes, too, following the color order required. This can only be done in patterns where you are using two ends as one.

There are a number of ways to work with a doubled warp and weft. No matter which method you choose, wind your threads with even tension on both threads. Mini cones are an excellent put-up for this purpose. Use two cones of the same color when winding your warp or weft. It decreases your warping time because you are threading two ends at a time. It also allows you to manage the two yarns easily. If you purchased your yarn on a single large cone, you can wind off a center-pull ball and use the cone and ball as separate yarn supplies. You can also pull from both ends of a center-pull ball.

If you are using two threads of weft, wind them evenly, applying equal tension to both threads so that they come off the shuttle or bobbin at the same rate.

warp ends beyond the other ply.

Press the weft into place. Add in your new color, joining it at the selvedge as you did with the old. Leave the tails in place and cut them flush with the cloth after washing.

BOAT SHUTTLES

If you're weaving with fine yarn or managing multiple colors that change frequently, a boat shuttle can be very handy. Wind a bobbin with each color and then swap out the bobbins as you work.

Bobbins should be wound with the yarn under moderate tension and so that the yarn builds up on the bobbin evenly and smoothly. Lumps or soft spots will cause your yarn to wind off with a jerky motion.

To wind a tidy bobbin, place the yarn supply on the floor or in a cone holder to allow the weft to travel in a straight line from the supply to the working action of the winder. Holding the yarn under just moderate tension, guide the yarn back and forth with your hand to evenly fill the bobbin. Take care not to overfill so that the yarn spills over the lip of the bobbins.

Fixing Mistakes

No matter how careful you are, mistakes happen. Get in the habit of spot checking your work as you weave. If you spot a mistake, you have four choices. Ignore the mistake because no one will notice; unweave and fix it; cut it out and start anew; or fix it after the project is off the loom.

If I spot a mistake that I can't live with, I'll cut out the wefts and start weaving again. It saves lots of time and puts less wear and tear on the warp. To do this, take a sharp pair of embroidery scissors and carefully cut the weft down the middle. Pull out the cut yarns at the selvedge and start weaving over again.

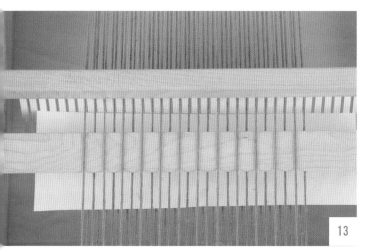

13

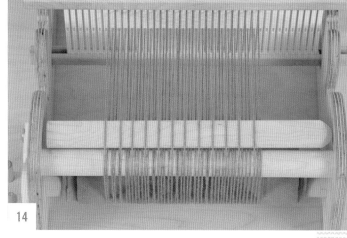

14

With the heddle in the down position, slide a piece of paper behind the heddle and between the down ends in the holes and the up ends in the slots to make it easier to pick up the correct threads.

When not in use, you can slide the pick-up stick to the back of the loom so it won't interfere with an up or down plainweave shed.

Pick-up Stick Primer

Many of the patterns in this book make use of one or more pick-up sticks. They are used to break the over/ under order of plain weave to create sections of warp that float over or under more than one warp or weft. Pick-up sticks come in a variety of shapes and sizes. A good pick-up stick will be sanded smooth so it doesn't snag the warp and will have at least one beveled end to allow you to easily pick up warp threads. The width of the pick-up stick will determine how tall your shed will be.

CATCHING YOUR SELVEDGES

Because pick-up patterns break the over/under configuration of plain weave, you will end up with floats at the selvedge. This may cause you to skip the selvedge when weaving the next pick. In these cases, you must manually pick up the selvedge thread in order to catch it.

WORKING IN FRONT OF THE HEDDLE

You can use pick-up sticks in front of or behind the rigid heddle. When picking up in front of the heddle, you have to pick up each row; tip the pick on its edge, place the weft, and then remove the stick before pressing the yarn into place.

WORKING BEHIND THE HEDDLE

When working with a single pick-up stick behind the rigid heddle, you don't have to remove the stick each time. You do, however, want to be sure that you only pick up the slot threads. To do this, place the rigid heddle in the down position so that only the slot threads are up. It may make it easier to see the warp threads to add a sheet of contrasting paper between the warp layers (photo 13). Working behind the heddle, pick up the slot threads indicated in the pick-up.

The patterns in this book will tell you how to load or charge the pick-up stick.

When not in use, push the pick-up stick to the back of the loom so that it doesn't interfere with the up plain weave shed (photo 14).

When reading a pick-up pattern, you will see two different kinds of instructions: "Pick-up stick" and "Up and pick-up stick."

"Pick-up stick" indicates that you should place the heddle in neutral, slide the pick-up stick forward, and tip it up on its edge, raising the threads on the stick above the warp (photo 15). This position creates a weft float.

For some styles of rigid-heddle looms, placing the heddle in neutral can be fiddly. If your loom doesn't allow you to place the heddle in neutral, you can let it hang in front of the heddle block and tip the pick-up stick on edge. Be sure that you have good tension on

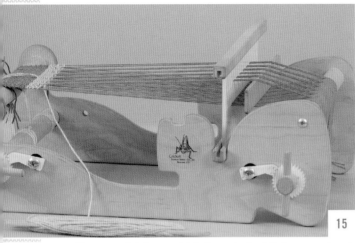

To weave "pick-up stick" place the heddle in neutral and tip the pick-up stick on its edge.

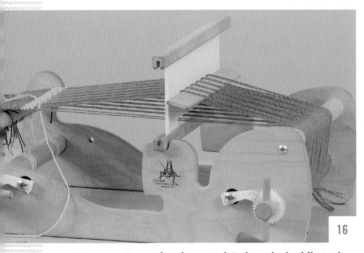

To weave "up and pick-up stick," place the heddle in the up position and slide the pick-up stick toward the back of the heddle.

the yarns, otherwise the heddle will interfere and you won't get a clean shed.

"Up and pick-up stick" indicates that you should place the heddle in the up position and slide the pick-up stick to the back of the rigid heddle (photo 16). This position creates a warp float.

Note when weaving a down shed in this position, you can leave the pick-up stick in place. You only need to push it to the back of the loom when weaving an up shed.

These skills, tools, and tips will come in handy for the rest of your weaving life. They are the techniques that I see solve so many of my student's issues when they struggle with making cloth they love. Prepared with this know-how, you can confidently go to the loom to weave.

PLACING A HEDDLE ROD

Several patterns in this book, such as the Twill and Tweed Pillow Cover, require using a second pick-up stick that is picked up in the opposite order as the first. If these warp ends are left on a pick-up stick, they will interfere with the warp ends on the first stick (photo 1).

By placing the warp ends on a heddle rod, they can be easily picked up without interfering with the first pick-up stick, at the same time eliminating the need to remove and recharge the pick-up stick every time. You will need a dowel or rod that is at least 2" (5 cm) longer than the width of your warp to be your heddle rod.

The appropriate warp ends will be attached to the rod via string heddles. These are small loops of yarn that slide under the warp threads and attach the warp ends to the rod, allowing you to lift them up to make an appropriate shed.

Start by making a string heddle for every end you are going to pick up, using your rigid heddle as a guide (photo 2). Sturdy smooth cotton, such as crochet or mercerized cotton, works best. Tie the string around the heddle, then tie a sturdy square knot. Cut the string and then wrap and tie another heddle. Continue working in this manner until you have created enough string heddles for your project.

With the rigid heddle in the down position and working behind the rigid heddle, pick up the warp ends you wish to place on the rod. Bring the pick-up stick up close to the rigid heddle and set it on its edge so that it raises the picked-up warp ends. Take one of your string heddles and place it under the first lifted end. Fold it in half so that the string heddle encases the warp end and place both ends of the loop on the heddle rod. Take the next string heddle and place it under the picked up end(s) and place it on the heddle rod (photo 3). Continue in this manner until you have placed all of the string heddles on the heddle rod.

It is a good idea to secure the loops to the rod using painter's tape so that the rod doesn't slip out while you're weaving. Painter's tape isn't as sticky as duct or masking tape, so it will be easy to remove.

The heddle rod resides behind the rigid heddle and in front of the first pick-up stick. When the pattern calls for the heddle rod, lift up on the rod to engage those warp ends (photo 4). When not in use, it can rest behind the rigid heddle.

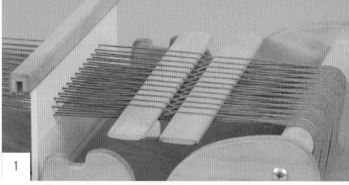

1

When working with more than one pick-up stick, it is possible they might interfere with one another. Using a heddle rod will eliminate this problem.

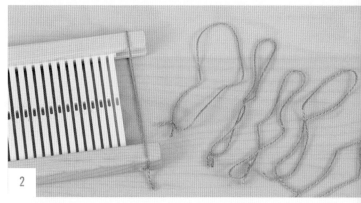

2

Use your rigid heddle as a guide to tie uniform string heddles.

3

Use the string heddles to secure the pick-up warp ends to a heddle rod.

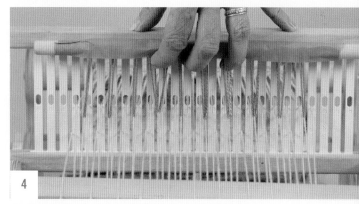

4

To engage the heddle rod, place the heddle in the appropriate position (up is shown), then pull up on the rod to lift the picked-up warp end.

CHAPTER THREE

FOLLOWING the PATTERNS

If you are relatively new to weaving, you might not be familiar with how to read a pattern. This chapter provides a short guide to the information given with each project in this book and describes how to make the best use of it.

Reading the Weaving Instructions

Each pattern has a list of project specs that details the information you need to set up and weave the pattern. This information includes everything from the finished size to the materials and equipment you'll need to gather, including:

FINISHED SIZE

This is the final finished size of the project after washing it.

WEAVE STRUCTURE

A weave structure is the interlacement that is formed via a specific setup or technique. Weave structures range from plain weave, in which the weft travels over 1 warp end and under the adjacent warp end, to more elaborate structures in which the weft travels over or under more than 1 warp end.

EQUIPMENT

This lists the size loom and rigid heddle you need to weave the project and the necessary accessories.

NOTIONS

This lists any additional tools or materials necessary to complete the project.

SETT

Sett is the weaver's gauge. It tells you how open or dense your warp spacing should be to weave the project successfully. It is expressed in a number that represents the number of ends of warp in 1" (2.5 cm), measured on the loom, to space the yarns.

WEAVING WIDTH

This measurement is the width of the warp in the rigid heddle. You use this number to center your project in the rigid heddle.

PICKS PER INCH (PPI)

This is the number of weft ends, called picks, that are in the woven cloth under tension on the loom. Paying attention to this number will ensure that your final cloth looks like the sample cloth in the picture.

WARP LENGTH

This measurement indicates the length of your warp.

NUMBER OF ENDS

This is the number of individual warp ends you need to wind for the project. .

YARNS

This section lists the yarns and amounts used in the project, as well as the colors and brand names. The information is listed in this order: the generic name of yarn, its fiber content, the yarn's yardage listed as yd (m)/lb, and the amount of each yarn you will need and in what colors. This generic yarn information is followed by details about the specific yarn used in the pattern, including the yarn maker, brand name, fiber content, yardage by put-up, and color names and numbers.

TIP: *When gathering your yarns, be sure you are looking at the project yardage number and not the yarn's yardage number.*

RECOMMENDED WARPING METHOD

Each project includes my recommendation for a warping method in the project specs. (See Chapter Nine for more information about warping techniques.)

Following Charts

There are two types of charts used in a number of the patterns. These charts offer an easy-to-read shorthand of how to thread the loom and weave the pattern.

WARP COLOR ORDER CHART

Read this chart from right to left. The number indicates how many warp ends to thread in a particular color before changing to a different color. Keep in mind that an "end" is a working end, which is 1 unit in a slot or hole. The chart key will tell you if there is more than 1 thread in a slot or hole. The chart will also indicate if it is important to start in a slot or a hole. The bracket at the top indicates how many times to repeat each sequence.

For instance, in the example chart (figure 1) from the Four Looks Kitchen Towels, you will thread 5 dark blue ends of 2 threads each, then 5 light blue ends of 2 threads each, etc. The note under the figure tells you the total number of ends, which also equals the total number of slots and holes and the total number of threads or individual yarns. The bracket indicates that you will repeat this sequence 7 times.

WEAVE COLOR ORDER CHART

Read this chart from top to bottom. It tells you the color order of your weaving, and each color is listed across the top, like in the example chart (figure 2). The number indicates how many picks of that color you will weave. If there is a bracket along the side, it indicates that the information within the brackets should be repeated a specific number of times.

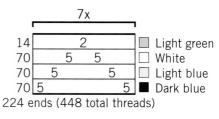

224 ends (448 total threads)

FIGURE 1

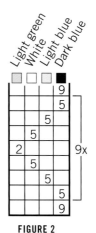

FIGURE 2

CHAPTER FOUR

THE KITCHEN

The kitchen is perhaps the most woven-for room in the house. The key to project weaving for the kitchen is to create fabrics that both wear well and dry easily. The humble kitchen towel, a favorite weaver's project, need not be so humble. When you make them with customized stripes, favorite plaids, or a bright hounds-tooth check, your handwoven towels turn everyday chores into daily pleasures. Weavers can decorate their kitchens from floor to (almost) the ceiling with café curtains and rag rugs, too.

Four Looks KITCHEN TOWELS

Striped warps are fun to play around with. From one warp, you can get many looks. Pair these striking plaid and stripe patterns with a highly absorbent mix of unmercerized cotton and cottolin yarns in a generously sized towel, and you get an everyday towel that will bring a smile every time you use it. Size them up or down according to the width of your loom or the needs of your kitchen.

PROJECT SPECS

FINISHED SIZE
Four towels, each 19½" x 28½" (49.5 x 72.5 cm).

WEAVE STRUCTURE
Plain weave.

EQUIPMENT
10-dent rigid-heddle loom with a 23" (58.5 cm) weaving width; 5 stick shuttles or a boat shuttle with 5 bobbins.

NOTIONS
Tapestry needle; sewing thread and needle; scrap yarn.

WARP AND WEFT SPECS

SETT (EPI)
10 (working ends are doubled threads in the heddle).

WEAVING WIDTH
22½" (57 cm).

PICKS PER INCH (PPI)
10 (using a doubled weft).

WARP LENGTH
4½ yd (4.1 m; includes 18" [45.7 cm] for loom waste and take-up).

NUMBER OF ENDS
224 ends (448 total threads used doubled).

RECOMMENDED WARPING METHOD
Indirect.

YARNS

Warp: 22/2 cottolin (3,246 yd [2,968 m]/lb): 630 yd (576 m) each light blue, dark blue; 8/2 unmercerized cotton (3,369 yd [3,081 m]/lb): 126 yd (115 m) light green, 630 yd (576 m) white.

Shown here: Louet North America 22/2 Organic Cottolin (60% cotton/40% linen; 710 yd [649 m] /3.5 oz mini cone): #24042 Light Blue, #25003 Kentucky Blue; Cotton Clouds Aurora Earth (100% unmercerized cotton; 890 yd [814 m] 4 oz mini cone): #45 Nile Green, #75 Bleach.

Weft: 22/2 cottolin: 452 yd (413 m) light blue; 858 yd (785 m) dark blue; 8/2 unmercerized cotton (3,369 yd [3,080 m]/lb): 72 yd (66 m) light green; 356 yd (326 m) white.

Shown here: Louet North America 22/2 Organic Cottolin: #24042 Light Blue, #25003 Kentucky Blue; Cotton Clouds Aurora Earth: #45 Nile Green, #75 Bleach.

Warping

1   Warp your loom following the project specs and the Warp Color Order chart, threading 2 ends in every slot and hole.

NOTE. *The indirect method of warping is recommended for this project because of the odd number of warp ends in the stripes. However, if you prefer the direct method, it can be warped easily by threading both the holes and slots at the same time. Simply pull loops of yarn through the heddle and to the warping peg. This method can only be used in patterns like this one when you are using 2 ends of the same yarn as 1.*

Weaving

2   Wind 4 shuttles or bobbins with doubled ends of each weft color and a fifth shuttle or bobbin with scrap yarn. (See Chapter Two for tips on winding and weaving with doubled wefts.)

3   Weave a 1" (2.5 cm) header of scrap yarn to spread your warp (see Chapter Two).

4   Begin the first towel by leaving a tail 6 times the weaving width. Weave 2" (5 cm) plain weave in the color indicated in the Weave Color Order chart.

5   Thread the tail in a tapestry needle and, using the hem or embroidery stitch (see Chapter Ten), secure the beginning of the weaving.

6   Continue to weave each of the 4 different towels following the Weave Color Order charts and using a double strand of weft for all picks.

     Finish each towel with hem or embroidery stitch, leave a 4" (10 cm) unwoven gap of warp, and then start the next towel, again leaving a long tail for hem or embroidery stitch.

WARP COLOR ORDER

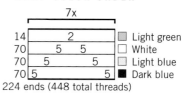

	7x			☐ Light green
14	2			☐ White
70	5	5		☐ Light blue
70	5		5	■ Dark blue
70	5		5	

224 ends (448 total threads)

WEAVE COLOR ORDER

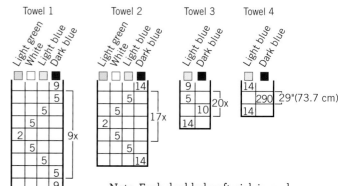

Note: Each doubled weft pick is made up of two yarns.

Finishing

7   Remove the cloth from the loom. Trim any tails to 2" (5 cm). Trim the fringe to ¼" (6 mm).

8   Fold the end over ¼" (6 mm), and then fold again ½" (1.3 cm) to encase the fringe. Pin the seam to secure for stitching. Using coordinating sewing thread, machine or whipstitch the fold in place (see Chapter Ten).

9   Machine wash towels on the gentle cycle in cool water with a regular detergent. Tumble dry on low and remove towels while still damp. Trim any weft tails flush with the fabric.

Fabric Stash RAG RUG

Rugs and rags, what could be better? This is one of the most versatile weaving materials because it isn't limited to your floor. Rags make great runners, placemats, and table squares. Keep an eye out at the thrift store or the sale rack for interesting fabrics that you can recycle into fodder for your loom. This rug incorporates stripes and checks for a clean, cheerful accent on your floor.

PROJECT SPECS

FINISHED SIZE
One 20½" x 36¼" (52 x 92 cm) rug.

WEAVE STRUCTURE
Plain weave.

EQUIPMENT
8-dent rigid-heddle loom with a 21" (53.5 cm) weaving width; four 20" (51 cm) stick shuttles; tapestry beater; sewing machine.

NOTIONS
Self-healing mat and rotary cutter; quilting ruler; sewing thread and needle; scrap yarn; two 3" (7.5 cm) S-hooks (optional).

WARP AND WEFT SPECIFICATIONS

SETT (EPI)
8.

WEAVING WIDTH
21" (53.5 cm).

PICKS PER INCH (PPI)
5.

WARP LENGTH
60" (152.5 cm; includes 18" [45.5 cm] for loom waste and take-up).

NUMBER OF ENDS
168.

RECOMMENDED WARPING METHOD
Direct.

YARNS

Warp: 8/4 cotton carpet warp (1,600 yd [1,463 m]/lb): 200 yd (183 m) dark green, 80 yd (73 m) pink.

Shown here: Cotton Clouds Rug Warp (100% unmercerized cotton, 800 yd [732 m]/8 oz cone): #15 Myrtle Green, #11 Peach.

Weft: 1½" (3.8 cm) bias-cut 100% cotton rag strips: 35 yd (32 m) green print, 75 yd (69 m) light yellow, 30 yd (27 m) aqua blue.

Shown here: 45" (114 cm) wide 100% cotton quilting fabric.

Warping

1 Warp your loom following the project specs and the Warp Color Order chart.

Weaving

2 Wind 3 shuttles with the rag weft strips and a fourth shuttle with scrap yarn.

3 Weave a 1" (2.5 cm) header of scrap yarn to spread your warp (see Chapter Two).

4 Starting with the patterned green rag weft and leaving a 4" (10 cm) tail, weave 1 pick. Open a second shed, tuck the tail into this shed 3" (7.5 cm), and allow the rest of the tail to exit the warp.

5 Continue weaving following the Weave Color Order chart.

   As you weave, pack the weft firmly with the rigid heddle.

   Stop every 1" (2.5 cm) with the heddle in position for the next shed—if you just wove an up shed, place the heddle in the down position or vice versa. Use a tapestry beater to firmly pack the weft. You will most likely compress the warp to half its height.

TIP: *If you run out of weft within a color strip, overlap the ends in the middle of the fabric, tapering each end to decrease bulk. To transition between one color and another, use the ply-splitting method to decrease bulk(see Chapter Two). To create the split, cut 10" (25.5 cm) of the end of the rag weft in half.*

   As you weave, maintain a generous weft angle to keep the selvedges from pulling in.

   You may notice some crowding of the selvedge threads. This can happen when weaving on an open sett. Use your finger to manually spread the threads closer to the selvedge occasionally. You may also find it helpful to weight the selvedge threads with S-hooks.

   If using a rag fabric that is printed only on one side, you may have to sometimes flip or tuck the fabric so that the face of the rug mostly shows the face of the fabric; otherwise, you will have splotches of white fabric within the pattern areas.

WARP COLOR ORDER

48		24	24	▢	Pink
120	40	40	40	▣	Dark green

168 ends

WEAVE COLOR ORDER

Finishing

6 Remove the cloth from the loom, leaving 5" (12.5 cm) of warp on each end for tying fringe knots.

7 Finish with 2 rows of staggered overhand knots worked in groups of 4 warp ends. Remove the scrap yarn a few inches (or centimeters) at a time to keep the weft from working its way loose as you tie the knots.

8 Use a rotary cutter and self-healing mat to trim the fringe to ½" (1.3 cm) or your desired length. Trim any rag tails flush with the rug.

9 It isn't necessary to wash your rug before using. If it becomes soiled over time, machine wash on the gentle cycle.

Fabric Stash Rag Rug   **43**

SELECTING, PREPARING, AND CUTTING FABRIC FOR RAG RUG WEFT

Almost any type of fabric will work for making the Rag Rug. I prefer working with yardage off the bolt rather than discarded clothing because there are no lumpy seams to deal with. I look for fabric with interesting patterns on the front and back. You can use a wide variety of fabric types, including wool, rayon, cotton, and cotton-poly blends.

Wash and dry your fabric first to remove any sizing and to make the rags easier to compress. It isn't necessary to press the fabric after washing.

Cutting Your Fabric

There are many ways to cut or rip rags for weaving. If you are ripping strips for rags, start with an extremely long piece of fabric, 3–5 yd (2.7–3.7 m) long. Lay it so that the cut end is facing you, then make a small cut every 1½" (3.8 cm) along the width of the end. Rip the fabric at these cuts to create long strips of fabric.

My preferred method is to cut them on the bias so that the edges are less likely to fray. Plus, you can create an extremely long piece of continuous rag weft. If you are familiar with making bias tape, this is a similar method on a much larger scale.

1   Fold in half 2 yd (1.8 m) of fabric. Using coordinating sewing thread and the straight stitch, machine sew the 3 raw sides together, leaving ½" (1.3 cm) seam allowance.

2   Lay the fabric on a flat surface with the fold on your left. Using a sharp pair of scissors, cut a small slit inside the seam through the top layer of fabric, being careful not to cut the stitching and just the top layer. Insert your scissors and cut just the top layer from the bottom right corner to the top left corner, stopping just before the stitching (figure 1).

3   Flip the fabric over, keeping the fold on your left, and cut through the top layer—it was the bottom layer during the first cut—from the bottom left corner to the top right corner (figure 2).

4   Place your left hand in the middle of the left side of the upper layer cut line and your right hand in the middle of the right side the upper cut line (figure 3).

Lift the fabric off the table so that the fabric forms a tube (figure 4).

Fold the fabric over lengthwise so that the right fold stops 4" (10 cm) shy of the left fold (figure 5).

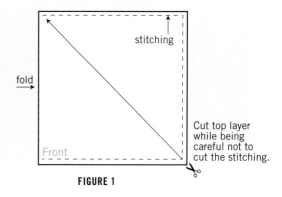

FIGURE 1

fold

stitching

Front

Cut top layer while being careful not to cut the stitching.

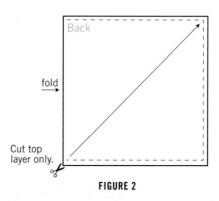

FIGURE 2

Back

fold

Cut top layer only.

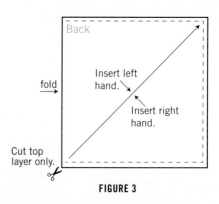

FIGURE 3

Back

fold

Insert left hand.

Insert right hand.

Cut top layer only.

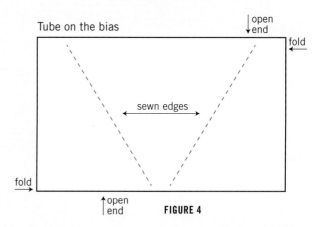

FIGURE 4

Tube on the bias

open end

fold

sewn edges

fold

open end

5 Using a self-healing mat, rotary cutter, and quilting ruler, cut away the raw edges and even the sides. Cut the fabric in 1½" (3.8 cm) strips, starting from the right fold and stopping 3" (7.5 cm) from the left fold (figure 6).

6 Place your left arm inside the tube formed at the left side fold and lift the fabric off the table. You will have a solid piece of fabric on your arm and loops of 1½" (3.8 cm) fabric hanging down from the top fold. This is often called a bias tape hula (figure 7).

Cut the fabric strips at an angle so that they form a continuous strip of bias tape. To do this, roll your arm so that your palm is facing the ground and the fold of solid cloth is facing you on the top of your arm. The first cut is the most important! If you cut straight across, you will have loops of fabric fall to the floor. Start by cutting the first strip at an angle from the middle of the fold to the left side of the first strip of fabric (figure 8). Let this strip fall to the ground.

7 Next, working carefully so as not to nick your arm, cut from the outer edge of the right strip still on your arm to the outer edge of the strip on the other side of the fold.

8 Continue cutting in this manner until you have cut all the strips from your hand. The last cut will go from the lower strip to the middle of the fold. Let the strips fall to the ground as you work.

9 You now have a pile of continuous strips on the floor. Wind the fabric in a ball or straight onto your shuttle.

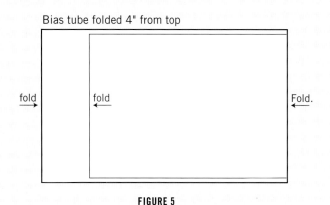

Bias tube folded 4" from top

fold · fold · Fold.

FIGURE 5

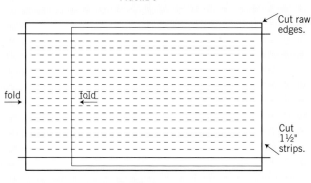

fold · fold

Cut raw edges.

Cut 1½" strips.

FIGURE 6

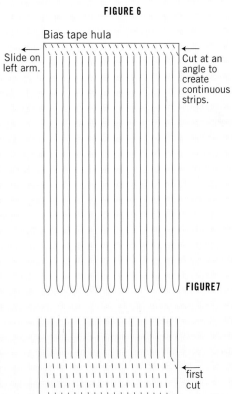

Bias tape hula

Slide on left arm.

Cut at an angle to create continuous strips.

FIGURE 7

first cut

fold

FIGURE 8

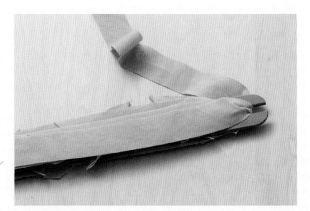

Specialized shuttles used for rag weaving allow you to efficiently pack on a lot of bulky wefts. But most of these shuttles are too tall for the relatively small shed that a rigid-heddle loom produces. I used a stick shuttle and wound my rags on as flat as possible around the middle of the shuttle. Because you are weaving relatively short repeats, you don't need a specialized tool to get the job done.

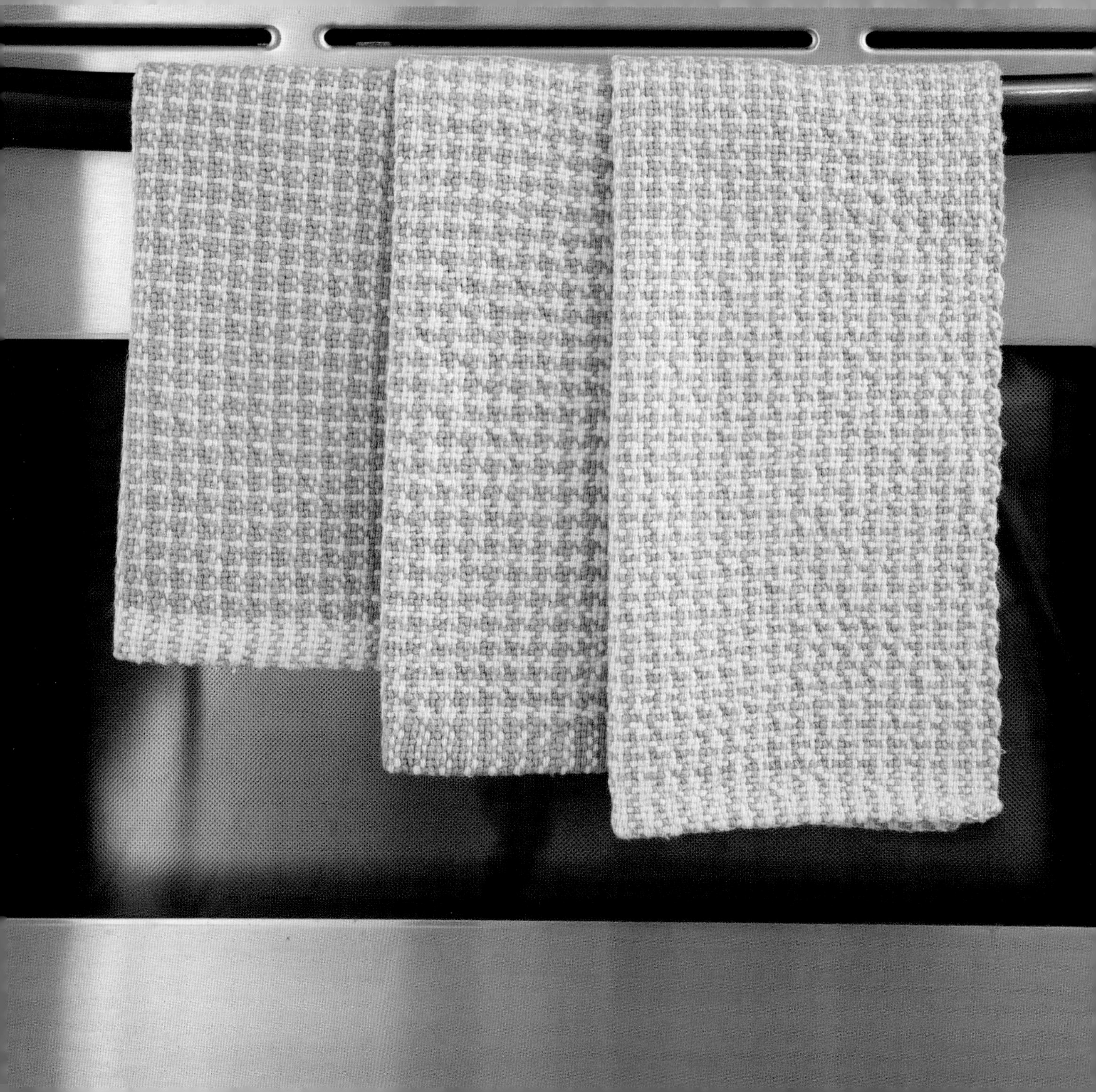

Light Bright **TOWELS**

These cheerful towels work up quickly. From one warp, you can get several looks using the magic of color-and-weave. Color-and-weave is a plain weave structure that alternates light and dark yarns in differing combinations to create seemingly complex structures. It's all optics! In a chunky cotton, you can weave up in one weekend a stack of towels that will brighten any kitchen and impress your guests.

PROJECT SPECS

FINISHED SIZE
Three towels, each 13¼" x 19½" (33.5 x 49.5 cm).

WEAVE STRUCTURE
Color-and-weave.

EQUIPMENT
8-dent rigid-heddle loom with a 15" (38.1 cm) weaving width; 4 stick shuttles.

NOTIONS
Sewing thread and needle; scrap yarn.

WARP AND WEFT SPECIFICATIONS

SETT (EPI)
8.

WEAVING WIDTH
15" (38 cm).

PICKS PER INCH (PPI)
8.

WARP LENGTH
97" (246 cm; includes 24" [45.5 cm] for loom waste, take-up, and interstitial fringe).

NUMBER OF ENDS
118.

RECOMMENDED WARPING METHOD
Direct.

YARNS

Warp: 4-ply worsted-weight cotton (792 yd [724 m]/lb): 162 yd (148 m) pink, 157 yd (144 m) yellow.

Shown here: Lion Brand Yarns Kitchen Cotton (100% cotton, 99 yd [91 m]/2 oz): #103 Bubblegum, #157 Citrus.

Weft: 4-ply worsted-weight cotton: 138 yd (126 m) pink, 108 yd (99 m) yellow; 8/2 unmercerized cotton (3,360 yd [3,070 m]): 26 yd (24 m) pink, 22 yd (20 m) pink, 43 yd (39 m) yellow.

Shown here: Lion Brand Yarns Kitchen Cotton: #103 Bubblegum, #157 Citrus, Cotton Clouds Aurora Earth, #32 Maize, #24 Beauty Rose.

Warping

1   Warp your loom following the project specs. Start with 2 pink ends, then alternate 2 yellow and 2 pink ends across the warp 29 times for a total of 118 ends (60 pink and 58 yellow).

Weaving

2   Wind 1 shuttle with each color of weft and 1 with a smooth, chunky scrap yarn.

3   Weave a 1" (2.5 cm) header of scrap yarn to spread your warp.

4   Begin and end each towel with 15 picks, about 1½" (3.8 cm) of the 8/2 weft, allowing for your preferred method of hemming (see Chapter Ten).

5   Continue to weave the towels following the Weave Color Order chart, leaving a 2" (5 cm) gap of unwoven warp between towels. Be mindful of managing your selvedges as you exchange colors (see Chapter Two).

Finishing

6   Remove the cloth from the loom. Trim any tails to 2" (5 cm). Trim the fringe to ¼" (6 mm).

7   Fold the end over ¼" (6 mm), then fold again ½" (1.3 cm) to encase the fringe. Line up the folded edge with the transition from solid color to pattern, taking care that the weaving done with 8/2 cotton is on the back. Pin the seam to secure for stitching and press. Using coordinating sewing thread, machine stitch or whipstitch the fold in place.

8   Machine wash the towels on the gentle cycle in cool water with laundry detergent.

9   Tumble dry on low and remove towels while still damp. Trim any weft tails flush with the fabric.

WEAVE COLOR ORDER

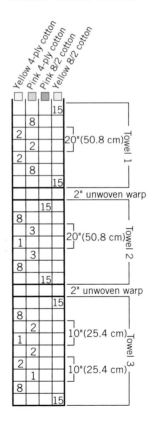

Fresh Baked Bread CLOTH

This is the kind of cloth that inspired the term "linens." Finely woven from quality linen yarn, it will wear like iron. With two heddles, you can weave fine cloth, like this one, with amazing drape and add sweet pattern accents that you can weave without using pick-up sticks.

PROJECT SPECS

FINISHED SIZE
One 22" x 29" (56 x 74 cm) cloth.

WEAVE STRUCTURES
Plain weave with English Plain Weave and Bird's Eye Twill.

EQUIPMENT
Rigid-heddle loom with a 24" (61 cm) weaving width; two 10-dent rigid heddles; 3 stick shuttles; warping sticks.

NOTIONS
Tapestry needle; sewing thread and needle; scrap yarn.

WARP AND WEFT SPECIFICATIONS

SETT (EPI)
20.

WEAVING WIDTH
24" (61 cm).

PICKS PER INCH (PPI)
10 plain weave; 15 pattern.

WARP LENGTH
50" (127 cm; includes 18" [45.5 cm] for loom waste and take-up).

NUMBER OF ENDS
480.

RECOMMENDED WARPING METHOD
Indirect 2-Heddle

YARNS

Warp: 16/2 dry-spun linen (2,400 yd [2,195 m]/lb): 668 yd (610 m) green.

Shown here: Halcyon Newport Linen (100% dry-spun linen, 2,400 yd [2,195 m]/lb): #2370 Green.

Weft: 16/2 dry spun linen: 240 yd (220 m) green, 38 yd (35 m) pink.

Shown here: Halcyon Newport Linen: #2370 Green, #2060 Pink.

Warping

1   Warp your loom using 2 heddles, following the project specs. (See Chapter Nine for tips on warping wide warps.)

Weaving

2   Wind 1 shuttle with the green ground weft yarn, 1 shuttle with the pink pattern weft yarn, and 1 shuttle with scrap yarn.

3   Weave a 1" (2.5 cm) header of scrap yarn to spread your warp.

4   Leaving a tail 6 times the weaving width, weave 2" (5 cm) plain weave. Pack the weft firmly as you weave by pressing firmly with the rigid heddle. You may notice that the plain weave areas look uneven on the loom. Three threads may be clumped together while one stands apart. Once washed, the fabric will even out.

5   Thread the tail in a tapestry needle and use the hem or embroidery stitch to secure the beginning of the weaving.

6   Weave another 4" (10 cm) plain weave for a total of 6" (15 cm) as shown in the Weave Color Order chart.

PATTERN REPEAT

7   Continue to follow the Twill Pattern Sequence list for the English Plain Weave and the Bird's Eye Twill patterns as well as the Weave Order chart. Within the pattern sequence area, carry the non-working weft yarn along the selvedge.

    When you have finished each pattern area, cut the pattern weft, leaving a 6" (15 cm) tail, and tuck the tail into the next shed of plain weave.

8   When you have finished weaving the pattern sequence 4 times and have woven the final 6" (15 cm) of plain weave, secure the end of the cloth with hem or embroidery stitch.

WEAVE COLOR ORDER

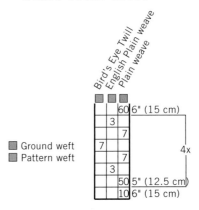

☐ Ground weft
☐ Pattern weft

TWILL PATTERN SEQUENCE

English Plain Weave (pattern weft)

1   Heddle 1 up.
2   Heddle 2 down.
3   Heddle 1 up.

Bird's Eye Twill (pattern weft)

1   Heddle 1 up.
2   Heddle 2 up.
3   Heddle 1 down.
4   Heddle 2 down.
5   Heddle 1 down.
6   Heddle 2 up.
7   Heddle 1 up.

WEAVING WITH LINEN

Linen is the ultimate luxury fiber for the home. Highly absorbent and cool to the touch, with a unique drape and a crisp hand, its durability and luster make linen prized for heirloom-quality table linens and curtains.

Its greatest strength is also its greatest weakness. It is made of bast fibers from the stem of the flax plant, which give the plant strength and stability. Its extremely long fiber length and stable nature create a yarn that has almost no elasticity. This is also why it is prone to wrinkle.

Warping

Linen's lack of rebound presents weavers with certain challenges. It requires tight and even tension, so when warping you need to treat the warp as a whole and not rake the fibers while winding on. Let the rigid heddle do the work. When pulling up the slack in the warp as you wind on the back beam, provide strong, steady tension on the entire warp, being careful not to pull on individual warp ends.

One of the few instances that I recommend using warping sticks instead of paper as a packing material is when weaving with linen. Warping sticks are laid between the warp layers as you wind onto the back beam at regular intervals. Paper can give way ever so slightly under the tension of the warp, but wood doesn't. This give can lead to soft spots in linen that won't show up with most other fibers.

Selvedges

When weaving with linen, keep an extra-close eye on the selvedges because crowding can cause them to break. To prevent crowding, maintain a consistent weft angle appropriate for your width of fabric. Advance the fabric every 2" (5 cm) to keep the weaving action in the area where the shed angle is low. Weighting the selvedges is also a good idea. Using a temple can be extremely helpful in maintaining the width of the fabric between pattern and plain weave areas (see Chapter Two).

Don't despair if you develop soft spots in your warp or if individual threads become loose; weight them using an S-hook and add additional weight if necessary. There is no shame in having a dozen hooks hanging off the back of your warp!

When linen fabric is fresh off the loom (this is called the "loom state"), it can look nothing like the finished cloth, particularly when you are using 2 heddles. This is called "rigid heddle" or "reed" marks. Because of linen's inelasticity, the 3 yarns that travel through the front slot clump together.

Finishing

Linen will completely transform in the wash. Linen likes a rough finish, so machine wash your project on the regular cycle with laundry detergent. It benefits from extra agitation, so some folks add in a terry-cloth towel or even tennis shoes. Then machine dry the entire load—towels and all—but remove your weaving while it's still damp. Press with a hot iron to bring out the shine in the yarn.

If you are new to working with linen, start with a small project and work your way up to a larger project, or consider using a less expensive and more elastic yarn blend such as cottolin.

Hemming

9   Remove the cloth from the loom. Trim any tails to 2" (5 cm). Trim the fringe to ½" (1.3 cm).

10 The side of the cloth that was facing you as you wove it is the front of the cloth. Turn the cloth over so the back faces you. Fold the end over a few picks below the fringe, then fold again ½" (1.3 cm) to encase the fringe and press. Pin the seam to secure for stitching. Using coordinating sewing thread, machine or whipstitch the fold in place.

Finishing

11 Machine wash your cloth on a regular cycle using hot water and laundry detergent, including a terry-cloth towel to provide additional agitation.
Tumble dry on low and remove while still damp.

12 Press immediately with a hot iron to bring out the shine in the linen yarn. Trim any remaining tails flush with the cloth.

Linen & Lace CAFÉ CURTAINS

Light streaming through linen is mesmerizing. Made from narrow panels that you can finish off in multiple ways, these lacy curtains will brighten up any room. Use this all-over pattern or weave lace borders on a plain weave ground. With this pattern as a guide, you can create lots of creative window treatments with your rigid-heddle loom, regardless of the width of your windows.

PROJECT SPECS

FINISHED SIZE
Four curtain panels, each 14" x 33" (35.5 x 84 cm) with 3" (7.5 cm) casings and 2" (5 cm) fringe.

WEAVE STRUCTURE
Honeycomb.

EQUIPMENT
10-dent rigid-heddle loom with a 15" (38 cm) weaving width; 2 shuttles; 16" (40.5 cm) pick-up stick; 16" (40.5 cm) heddle rod; 13 string heddles.

NOTIONS
Sewing thread and needle; self-healing mat and rotary cutter; scrap yarn; grommets or curtain clips (optional).

WARP AND WEFT SPECIFICATIONS

SETT (EPI)
10.

WEAVING WIDTH
15" (38 cm).

PICKS PER INCH (PPI)
10.

WARP LENGTH
5.5 yd (5 m; includes 38" [96.5 cm] for loom waste and take-up; loom waste includes interstitial fringe).

NUMBER OF ENDS
149.

RECOMMENDED WARPING METHOD
Indirect.

YARNS

Warp: 4-ply DK weight viscose linen blend (1,409 yd [1,288 m]/lb): 882 yd (807 m) indigo blue.

Shown here: Classic Elite Firefly (75% viscose/25% linen; 155 yd [142 m]/1¾ oz skein): #7793 Denim.

Weft: 4-ply DK weight viscose linen blend: 847 yd (775 m) light blue.

Shown here: Classic Elite Firefly: #7757 Chicory.

Warping

1   Warp your loom following the project specs. Start and end the warp in a hole. (See Chapter Nine for details on how to choose the best warping method and tips for winding long warps.)

Charging the Heddle Rod and Pick-Up Stick

First charge the heddle rod, then prepare the pick-up stick (see Chapter Two for how to make a heddle rod).

HEDDLE ROD

2   Place the heddle in the down position. Working behind the rigid heddle, pick up the slot threads: 1 up, [3 down/3 up x 12], 1 down.

3   Place the rigid heddle in neutral and tip the pick-up stick on its edge. Transfer the up threads to a heddle rod, wrapping a string heddle around each group of 3 up ends and the 1 up end at the beginning and placing the string heddles on the heddle rod.

PICK-UP STICK

4   Place the heddle in the down position. Working behind the rigid heddle, pick up the threads: 4 up, [(3 down/3 up) x11], 4 up. The pick-up stick should be behind the heddle rod.

Weaving

TIP: *The trick to weaving an all-over lace pattern that you plan to seam is making a plan for the pattern to line up—or, as in this case, offset, so you call as little attention to the seam as possible.*

This means that you need to work on maintaining a consistent beat so that the picks from one panel line up with the picks from the other. However, don't fret over this too much. With all-over lace, so much is going on that the eye will hardly notice if the patterns are slightly off at the seam.

5   To ensure that the panels are all the same size, make a paper guide, marking 33½" (85 cm) of pattern and 6½" (16.5 cm) of plain weave. Move and pin the guide to the fabric as you work. Each panel is woven from the bottom up, starting with the honeycomb pattern and ending with the plain weave casing.

6   Wind 1 shuttle with the weft yarn and 1 shuttle with scrap yarn.

7   Weave a 1" (2.5 cm) header of scrap yarn to spread your warp for the first panel and keep your weft in place until you are ready to work the finishing knots.

8   Weave 2 panels as follows, leaving 4" (10 cm) of warp between them:

Weave 2 picks of plain weave starting in the down position.

Weave 33½" (85 cm) in the honeycomb pattern following the Panel A Pattern. (See Chapter Two for tips on weaving warp and weft floats.)

9   Weave 6½" (16.5 cm) of plain weave.

10 Work a row of hemstitching to keep the weft in place during seaming.

11 Weave 2 more panels as you did the first, but start with 2 picks of plain weave and then reverse the order of the pick-up stick and heddle rod. This change in the pick-up pattern will offset the pattern at the selvedges for seaming. Follow the Panel B Pattern and leave 3" (10 cm) of warp between the panels.

12 Weave 6½" (16.5 cm) of plain weave, ending with a row of hemstitching.

Finishing

13   Remove the cloth from the loom. Cut the panels apart, leaving the fringes intact, and trim any tails to 2" (5 cm). Trim the warp to ¼" (6 mm) from the hemstitching after the plain weave areas.

JOIN TWO PANELS

14   To seam the 2 panels together, lay an A panel next to a B panel on a flat surface so that the plain weave headers line up and the pattern is offset at the seam.

TIP: *It is easier to make adjustments at the bottom of the curtain than it is at the top. If your panels don't quite line up at the bottom, you can remove a few picks until they do. For instance, if you have one more pattern repeat on one panel than the other, remove that repeat. You may have to remove the plain weave picks on the other panel so that they line up. The bottom will be a little wavy, but that just adds to the beauty of the curtain.*

15   Use the invisible seam stitch to join 2 panels (see Chapter Ten). Because this is a work of the hand, you may run into sections where the pattern doesn't quite line up; don't worry—it is far better to have the panels sewn together evenly without puckers than it is that the pattern lines up perfectly. Seams don't have to be seamless to be beautiful to the eye!

16   Repeat Steps 14 and 15 to join the 2 other panels.

PANEL A PATTERN

1   1 up.
2   Pick-up stick.
3   1 up.
4   Pick-up stick.
5   1 up.
6   Heddle rod.
7   1 up.
8   Heddle rod.

PANEL B PATTERN

1   1 up.
2   Heddle rod.
3   1 up.
4   Heddle rod.
5   1 up.
6   Pick-up stick.
7   1 up.
8   Pick-up stick.

Note: The patterns are woven upside down so that the weft floats are on top. This configuration allows you to engage the heddle rod easily and removes the necessity of having to pick up that row every time.

SEW THE CASING

17 Place the 2 sets of joined panels right side down; this is the side that was facing away from you as you wove. Fold the end over 2 picks below the fringe.

18 Finger press the fold in place or give it a light press with a steam iron on low.

   Fold again, so that the fold lines up with the last plain weave pick to make a 3" (7.5 cm) tube at the top of the curtain that encases the fringe. Pin the seam to secure for stitching.

   Using coordinating sewing thread, whipstitch the fold in place to complete the casing.

KNOT THE FRINGE

19 This finish mimics the oval shapes in the pattern. Remove the header and tie the fringe off in sets of 2 warp ends using an overhand knot (see Chapter Ten for knots instructions). Work 2 rows of Staggered Macramé Square Knots to make the fringe, using 2 ends as 1. Finish with a row of staggered overhand knots.

WASH THE PANELS

20 Fill a bathtub with lukewarm water and ⅛ cup of leave-in soap. Swish the water to mix in the soap and lay each panel in the tub flat, one on top of the other. Let soak for an hour.

21 Gently lift each panel out of the water, roll, and press with your hands to remove the water. Lay flat to dry on a clean towel.

22 Trim any remaining tails flush with the cloth. Trim fringe to desired length using a self-healing mat and a rotary cutter.

HANGING THE LINEN & LACE CAFÉ CURTAINS

Windows are the perfect frame to show off your handwovens, and you can hang your curtains in a few different ways. You can slip a curtain rod in the casing at the top of the panels (photo 1), whether they're seamed or hung singly, or you can add grommets for a curtain that is easy to push to the side of the curtain rod (photo 2).

Grommets are sold at any craft or sewing store. Simply follow the instructions on the package to install them. I like to run a line of sealant on the fabric, such as Fray Check, after I cut out the holes for the grommets.

Alternatively, you can buy clips that have curtain rod hangers built in (photo 3). These are great ways to display your handwoven curtains on your windows or your walls.

CHAPTER FIVE

THE DINING ROOM

Dare to dine! Bring back the sit-down meal by dressing your table with your beautiful handmade creations. From functional to fanciful, sitting down to a meal adorned with handwovens is always everyday treat. If you use the dining table as a workstation, create a designated space for your devices. In this chapter are mats, runners, napkins, and more that will make your table more than just a place to dump and run, but rather a space to live and linger.

Hemp HOT PADS

Working with nontraditional materials is a great way to work up quick projects. Experiment with chunky cord or rope that you can find at any craft or hardware store and combine it with any number of pick-up patterns. Start in the morning and by tea time, you'll have something new to tuck under your teapot.

PROJECT SPECS

FINISHED SIZE
Two hot pads, each 7" x 7" (17.8 cm x 17.8 cm) with 1" (2.5 cm) fringe.

WEAVE STRUCTURES
Pick-up lace and honeycomb.

EQUIPMENT
5-dent rigid-heddle loom with a 9" (23 cm) weaving width; 1 stick shuttle; 10" (25.5 cm) pick-up stick.

NOTIONS
Tapestry needle; scrap yarn (optional).

WARP AND WEFT SPECIFICATIONS

SETT (EPI)
5.

WEAVING WIDTH
8½" (21.5 cm).

PICKS PER INCH (PPI)
6.

WARP LENGTH
40" (102 cm; includes 23" [58 cm] for loom waste, take-up, and interstitial fringe).

NUMBER OF ENDS
41.

RECOMMENDED WARPING METHOD
Direct.

YARNS

Warp: Hemp cord (400 yd [366 m]/lb): 46 yd (42 m) tan.

Shown here: Darice Hemp (100% hemp, 67 yd [61 m]/8 oz ball): natural.

Weft: Hemp cord (400 yd [366 m]/lb): 25 yd (23 m) tan.

Shown here: Darice Hemp: natural.

Warping

1   Warp the loom following the project specs.

TIP: *Yarns that are thick and stiff, like the hemp cord shown, are likely to move easily around the apron rod.*

To keep the warp in place, tie a choke around the end of the warp. The warp must start and end in a slot to balance the pick-up patterns.

Weaving

2   Wind the shuttle with the weft yarn.

HOT PAD 1

NOTE: *This is one of the few projects in which weaving a header isn't necessary. The thick yarns should be fairly well spread out. However, if you prefer beating against a header, weave a few picks with a worsted weight scrap yarn.*

3   Charge pick-up stick A: Place the heddle in the down position. Pick up warp ends in the slots: 3 down/3 up 3 times, ending with 3 down.

4   Start in a down shed, and, leaving a 40" (101.5 cm) tail for hemstitching, weave 2 plain weave picks.

5   Weave the Hot Pad 1 Pattern once.

6   Thread the tail in the tapestry needle and work 1 row of hemstitching (see Chapter Ten) over 2 warp ends and 2 weft picks to the last 3 warp ends. Work a stitch over a single warp end and

2 weft ends. Finish by working the final 2 warp ends and 2 weft picks. Making this adjustment in the hemstitching takes into account the odd number of warp ends.

You may find it difficult to beat such large, stiff twine into place. Do your best to maintain an even beat and consistent number of picks. Because you are working a lace pattern, the yarns will move where they need to go after you take the project off the loom and wash it.

7   Repeat the Hot Pad 1 Pattern 5 more times.

8   End with 1 pick of plain weave and work 1 row of hemstitching as before.

HOT PAD 2

9   Leave 3" (7.5 cm) of warp between pads for fringe. Starting in a down position, weave 2 picks of plain weave, remembering again to leave a tail for hemstitching.

10   Weave 1 Hot Pad 2 Pattern repeat using pick-up stick A and hemstitch as for the first pad.

11   Charge pick-up stick B: Recharge the pick-up stick by reversing the order of the Hot Pad 2 Pattern pick-up pattern: 3 up/3 down, ending with 3 ends up.

12   Weave 1 pattern repeat using pick-up stick B.

13   Repeat the pick-up sequence in Steps 10–12 four more times, alternating between pick-up stick A and pick-up stick B.

14   End with a final round of the Hot Pad 2 Pattern using pick-up stick A.

15   Weave 3 picks of plain weave (down, up, down) and work 1 row of hemstitching as before.

Finishing

16 Remove the cloth from the loom and cut the 2 hot pads apart. Trim the fringe to 1" (2.5 cm).

17 Fill a basin large enough to submerge both mats with warm water. Soak the mats in water for at least an hour.

18 Lift them from the basin and allow the water to drain away from the cloth. Place the hot pads on a dry towel in the sunshine. This will both dry the mats and dissipate any musty odor that the twine may have picked up in processing.

HOT PAD 1 PATTERN

1 Down.

2 Up and pick-up stick.

3 Down.

4 Up and pick-up stick.

5 Down.

6 Up.

HOT PAD 2 PATTERN

1 Down.

2 Up and pick-up stick.

3 Down.

4 Up and pick-up stick.

Skip-a-Slot **PLACEMATS**

A chance mistake while sampling led to this fabric—sampling has its benefits! By skipping a slot every so often, you allow the weft to pop in these warp-dominate placemats without using a pick-up stick. The texture is created by alternating thick and thin picks and beating with a firm hand. This project is for all of you rigid-heddle weavers who like to play with color!

PROJECT SPECS

FINISHED SIZE
Two placemats, each 14¼" × 20" (36 x 51 cm).

WEAVE STRUCTURES
Crammed and spaced plain weave.

EQUIPMENT
12-dent rigid-heddle loom with a 16" (40.5 cm) weaving width; 12" (30.5 cm) stick shuttle or boat shuttle; 18" (45.5 cm) stick shuttle; tapestry beater.

NOTIONS
Sewing thread and needle; straight pins; tapestry needle; scrap yarn; two 3" (7.5 cm) S-hooks (optional).

WARP AND WEFT SPECIFICATIONS

SETT (EPI)
12 (2 ends in every hole and most slots, skipping slots as shown in the Warp Color Order chart).

WEAVING WIDTH
15" (38 cm).

PICKS PER INCH (PPI)
8.

WARP LENGTH
78" (198 cm; includes 24" [61 cm] for loom waste and take up).

NUMBER OF ENDS
169 ends (338 total threads, used doubled).

RECOMMENDED WARPING METHOD
Indirect.

YARNS

Weft: 3/2 mercerized cotton (1,260 yd [1,152 m]/lb): 170 yd (155 m) eachsilver blue, gray blue; 221 yd (202 m) turquoise, aqua each.

Shown here: Cotton Clouds Pearly Pearl (100% mercerized cotton, 1,260 yd [1,152 m]/lb cone): #55 Jade, #134 Cactus, #65 Crab, #60 Duck.

Weft: 3/2 mercerized cotton: 255 yd (233 m) maroon; 135 yd (123 m) coral.

Shown here: Cotton Clouds Pearly Pearl: #143 Raisin, #77 Dusty Coral.

Warping

1   Using the indirect warping method (which is recommended to best handle the frequent color changes), wind 91 pairs of the silver blue and grayblue threads and 78 pairs of the turquoise and aqua yarns threads, following the Warp Color Order chart.

     Start and end in a hole. Thread all holes with the silver-blue and grayblue combination and the slots with the turquoise and aqua combination, skipping slots as indicated in the chart.

NOTE: *The selvedges are both in a hole.*

Weaving

NOTE: *You are weaving this fabric upside down, so you won't see the maroon stripes created by the skipped slots on the face of the fabric. If you peek under your loom, you will see them.*

2   Wind your larger stick shuttle with 2 strands each of maroon and coral for a total of 4 threads. (See Chapter Two for tips on weaving with multiple threads.) This is your thick weft. Wind a second shuttle with 1 strand of maroon. This is your thin weft. Wind a third shuttle with scrap yarn and weave 2" – 3" (5–7.5 cm), beating firmly to spread your warp and provide a firm foundation for your fabric.

3   Leaving a tail 6 times the width of your warp, weave 1¾" (4.5 cm) of the thin weft.

4   Using the yarn tail and a tapestry needle and embroidery stitch (see Chapter Ten), secure the beginning of your cloth.

5   Alternate 1 thin and 1 thick weft for 22" (56 cm). Press each weft into place firmly, only occasionally using a tapestry beater to pack the weft into place (see Chapter Two).

TIP: *The threads on either side of the skipped slot may have slightly looser tension then the rest of the warp. If this becomes a problem, weight the loose pair of ends with an S-hook to add a bit of extra tension. It isn't likely to happen to every pair, but it always pays to keep a generous supply of S-hooks on hand. To weight the ends, slip the hook around the pair of ends at the back of the loom and allow it to hang off the back beam.*

6   End your first mat by weaving 1¾" (4.5 cm) of the thin pick. Secure the end of your cloth with embroidery stitch.

7   Leave a gap of 2" (5 cm) in the warp. Weave the second mat as you did the first.

Finishing

8   Remove the cloth from the loom. Cut the 2 mats apart and trim the fringe to ¼" (6 mm) from the embroidery stitch.

9   Fold the ends twice so that the fold meets the first thick pick. Using coordinating sewing thread and a sewing needle, whipstitch the fold in place.

10   Machine wash the mats on the gentle cycle and tumble dry on low. Steam-press if necessary. Trim any weft tails at their base where they meet the cloth.

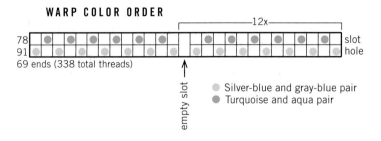

WARP COLOR ORDER

69 ends (338 total threads)

empty slot

○ Silver-blue and gray-blue pair
● Turquoise and aqua pair

Twill Be Done **RUNNER**

Twill can be woven one of two ways on a rigid-heddle loom; you can use two heddles or you can pick up the twill pattern in front of the loom as demonstrated in this project. You can weave any twill, and for that matter, any pattern, by picking up the pattern row by row in the front of the heddle. This is an excellent way to add texture and visual interest to your projects. Twills follow a nice step progression as they grow, and it's easy to get into the rhythm. The two twills used in this runner are reversible.

PROJECT SPECS

FINISHED SIZE
One 11½" x 38" (29 x 96.5 cm) runner with 1" (2.5 cm) fringe.

WEAVE STRUCTURES
Twill and plain weave.

EQUIPMENT
8-dent rigid-heddle loom with a 14" (35.5 cm) weaving width; 3 stick shuttles; 16" (40.5 cm) pick-up stick.

NOTIONS
Tapestry needle; rotary cutter and self-healing mat; scrap yarn.

WARP AND WEFT SPECIFICATIONS

SETT (EPI)
8.

WEAVING WIDTH
13¾" (35 cm).

PICKS PER INCH (PPI)
8 plain weave; 9 twill.

WARP LENGTH
64" (163 cm; includes 24" [61 cm] for loom waste and take-up).

NUMBER OF ENDS
106.

RECOMMENDED WARPING METHOD
Direct.

YARNS

Warp: 2-ply worsted weight recycled cotton (1,001 yd [915 m]/lb): 189 yd (173 m) blue green.

Shown here: Berroco Indigo (95% recycled cotton/5% other recycled fibers, 219 yd [200 m]/3½ oz skein): #6432 High-rise.

Weft: 4-ply worsted weight cotton/linen blend (1,001 yd [915 m]/lb): 123 yd (112 m) teal; 27 yd (25 m) yellow green.

Shown here: Rowan Creative Linen (50% cotton/50% linen, 219 yd [200 m]/3½ oz skein): #625 Teal, #629 Apple.

Warping

1   Warp your loom following the project specs.

Weaving

2   Wind the first shuttle with the teal ground weft, the second shuttle with the yellow green pattern weft, and the third shuttle with scrap yarn.

3   Weave a 1" (2.5 cm) header of scrap yarn to spread your warp (see Chapter Two).

4   Leaving a 4" (10 cm) tail, weave 1 pick with the ground weft. Open a second shed, tuck the tail into this shed 2" (5 cm), and allow the rest of the tail to exit the warp.

5   Weave 2 more picks. Start the twill pattern repeat as shown in the Weave Color Order chart and the twill pattern box, using the yellow-green yarn as your pattern weft.

6   After you have completed the twill pattern repeat at the beginning of the weaving, use the yellow-green pattern weft to work a row of clove-hitch knots (see Chapter Ten) at the beginning of the runner.

7   Weave the plain weave center of the runner as shown in the Weave Color Order chart, then weave the second twill pattern repeat in the same way as at the beginning of the runner.

   End with 3 picks of ground weft and 1 row of clove-hitch knots in the yellow-green pattern weft.

Finishing

8   Remove the cloth from the loom. Trim any tails to 2" (5 cm).

9   Fill a bathtub or large container with 3" (7.5 cm) of lukewarm water. Add ⅛ cup mild or no-rinse detergent. Slip the runner into the water, then gently swish it to help facilitate the floats to move into position. Allow to soak for 20 minutes.

10 Remove the runner from the water, holding it over the tub for a minute to let the excess water flow out. Roll it in a towel and press—don't wring—to remove any additional water. Dry flat on a clean towel.

11 Using a rotary cutter and self-healing mat, trim fringe to the desired length. Use a sharp pair of scissors to trim any tails flush with the cloth.

WEAVE COLOR ORDER

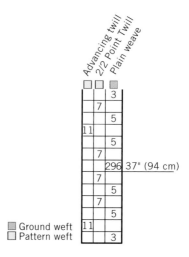

WEAVING TWILL IN FRONT OF THE HEDDLE

Each pattern repeat is stair-stepped over to create the iconic diagonal lines that make up twill. When weaving twill, I recommend that you catch the selvedge thread on every pick to maintain a tidy edge. You may have to break the pattern to do this .

Use a pick-up stick to pick up each row in front of the rigid heddle according to the pattern. Maintain a generous weft angle as twill has a tendency to draw in. You may find it helpful to use a temple (see Chapter Two).

End your ground weft and start each pattern repeat using the ply-splitting technique (see Chapter Two) or tuck in your beginning and ending tails as you weave.

2/2 POINT TWILL

Work in front of the heddle on a closed shed, from right to left:

ROW 1: Pick up: *over 2, under 2*, repeat *-*26 times; end with over 1, under 1.

ROW 2: Pick up: under 1, *over 2, under 2*, repeat *-*26 times; end with over 1.

ROW 3: Pick up: *under 2, over 2*, repeat *-*26 times; end with under 1, over 1.

ROW 4: Pick up: over 1*under 2, over 2*, repeat *-*26 times; end with under 1.

ROW 5: Repeat Row 3.

ROW 6: Repeat Row 2.

ROW 7: Repeat Row 1.

Advancing Twill Pattern

Work from right to left:

ROW 1: Pick up: over 1, under 1, *over 1, under 1, over 3, under 3*, repeat *-*13 times.

ROW 2: Pick up: over 1, under 2, *over 1, under 1, over 3, under 3*, repeat *-*12 times; end over 1, under 1, over 3, under 1, over 1.

ROW 3: Pick up: over 1, under 3, *over 1, under 1, over 3, under 3*, repeat *-* 12 times; end over 1, under 1, over 3, under 1.

ROW 4: Pick up: under 1, over 1, under 3, *over 1, under 1, over 3, under 3*, repeat *-*12 times; end over 1, under 1, over 3.

ROW 5: Pick up: over 3, under 3, *over 1, under 1, over 3, under 3*, repeat *-*12 times; end; over 1, under 3.

ROW 6: Pick up: under 1, over 3 under 3 *over 1, under 1, over 3, under 3*, repeat *-*12 times; end, over 1, under 2.

ROW 7: Pick up: *over 1, under 1, over 3, under 3* repeat *-*13 times; end over 1, under 1.

ROW 8: Pick up: under 1, *over 1, under 1, over 3, under 3*, repeat *-*13 times, over 1.

ROW 9: Repeat row 1.

ROW 10: Repeat row 2.

ROW 11: Repeat row 3.

READING A WEAVING DRAFT

A draft is a form of shorthand for weavers that is written with the floor loom weaver in mind. With a little know-how, rigid-heddle weavers can use this shorthand to create a chart. This chart can be used to as a guide to pick-up patterns in front of the heddle using a pick-up stick.

Parts of a Draft

Let's look at the draft that could be used for the 2/2 Point Twill Pattern used in the Twill Be Done Runner. All drafts share three components: threading, tie-up, and treadling.

The threading area shows how to thread the heddles. This is a draft for a 4-shaft loom which is indicated by the four rows. Each number represents a shaft on a floor or table loom. A rigid-heddle is essentially a 2-shaft loom. The first two "shafts" 1 and 2 are akin to a hole (1) and slot (2). Adding a second heddle adds more options, but they are not exactly the same. (See Chapter 9 for more information on the relationship between two heddles and four shafts.)

The tie-up area shows how to tie up the shafts to the treadles/levers of these other looms. This is akin to the heddle position of a rigid-heddle loom. Either the shaft is up or the shaft is down.

The treadling area shows the order to lift or lower the shafts to weave your pattern.

The fourth part to a draft is called a drawdown, which is often left off. It is a drawing of what the pattern will look like, generally shown underneath the threading and to the left of the treadling areas.

By drawing this part out, you can create an easy-to-read chart. It is helpful to draw this on graph paper or to photocopy the draft and draw in a grid that follows the lines of the draft in the blank area under the threading.

CREATING A DRAWDOWN

The goal is to draw in each of the treadling sequences line by line. Start by following the column indicated by the first treadling mark, in this case a circle, up to the tie-up area. In each area where there is a mark, an x in this case, look to the left and see which shaft is tied up to this treadle. You will then color in the square that is under this shaft and that lines up with the treadling mark. This is indicated by the arrows in the draft example. .

A second shaft is tied to this treadle, so you will also draw it in on that same line as the other colored box.

Continue working row by row until you have drawn in all of the areas indicated by the treadling marks. You will soon see a chart that actually looks like the pattern it weaves.

To use this chart, imagine that each row is a warp yarn and each column is a weft pick. Using a pick-up stick in front of the heddle and reading from top to bottom, pick up each warp end indicated by a colored square with your pick-up stick and allow the stick to float over the ends that are not colored in.

This chart shows you two repeats of the pattern, which is helpful because you can see how the pattern will grow. You need to repeat the pattern over and over again until you have worked from one edge of the weaving to the other.

You may come across drafts that look different than this example. They all will still have the same three parts, even if they are in different places or if they use different symbols. Not all drafts assume that if you step on a treadle the shafts will rise—in some cases, they sink! If for some reason your pattern doesn't look like the cloth pictured with the draft, take a peek underneath the loom, and I bet it will appear there.

Once you learn this trick, there is no weaving draft you can't use! There are entire books written about drafting and wonderful collections of weaving patterns to explore using this technique.

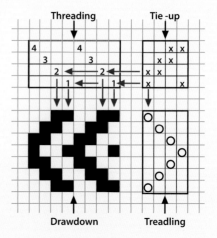

2/2 POINT TWILL PATTERN DRAFT

Four-Sided FRINGE NAPKINS

These napkins provide a no-fuss selvedge solution with fringe on all four sides. They have a terrific hand that is imparted by the close sett of a fine yarn, which creates a slightly warp-faced fabric that gives the appearance of solid stripes. If you do not have a double-heddle block, you can double the threads in a single heddle for a slightly different color effect and hand.

PROJECT SPECS

FINISHED SIZE
Four napkins, each 14" x 13" (35.5 cm x 33 cm) with ¼" (6 mm) fringe on all 4 sides.

WEAVE STRUCTURE
Warp-emphasis plain weave.

EQUIPMENT
Rigid-heddle loom with 16" (40.5 cm) weaving width; two 12-dent rigid heddles; 2 boat shuttles; 5 bobbins; sewing machine.

NOTIONS
Self-healing mat and rotary cutter; sewing thread; scrap yarn.

WARP AND WEFT SPECIFICATIONS

SETT (EPI)
24.

WEAVING WIDTH
15¾" (40 cm).

PICKS PER INCH (PPI)
14.

WARP LENGTH
89" (226 cm; includes 32" [81.5 cm] for loom waste and take-up, and interstitial fringe).

NUMBER OF ENDS
376.

RECOMMENDED WARPING METHOD
Direct 2-Heddle.

YARNS

Warp: 22/2 cottolin (3,246 yd [2,968 m]/lb): 228 yd (208 m) blue; 268 yd (245 m) yellow green; 158 yd (144 m) light green; 278 yd (254 m) yellow.

Shown here: Louet North America 22/2 Organic Cottolin (60% cotton/40% linen 710 yd [649 m]/ 3½ oz cone): #24042 Light Blue, #25053 Fern Green, #25051 Light Green, #21021 Very Light Yellow.

Weft: 22/2 cottolin: 95 yd (87 m) each blue, yellow green, light green, yellow.

Shown here: Louet North America 22/2 Organic Cottolin: #24042 Light Blue, #25053 Fern Green, #25051 Light Green, #21021 Very Light Yellow.

Warping

1 Warp your loom following the project specs and the Warp Color Order chart.

Weaving

NOTE: *Each napkin is woven with a different-colored weft. This shifts the colors and creates a different-colored side fringe in each one.*

2 Wind a bobbin with each of the 4 weft colors and 1 stick shuttle or bobbin with scrap yarn.

TIP: *When weaving with fine threads, I prefer to use a boat shuttle, which slides nicely across a fine, tight warp and makes it easy to swap out colors. If you don't have boat shuttles for this project, you can use stick shuttles instead.*

3 Weave a 1" (2.5 cm) header of scrap yarn to spread your warp (see Chapter Two).

4 To weave the first napkin, select a weft color and weave 14¼" (36 cm).

5 Weave 3" (7.5 cm) of scrap yarn between each napkin.

6 Using a different weft color for each one, repeat Steps 3–5 to weave 3 more napkins.

NOTE: *The fabric will look open on the loom with 3 ends clumped together and one end pushed apart from the others. This is caused by the spacing in the 2 heddles and is referred to as "reed marks." Don't worry; it will all come out in the wash. After the fabric is wet-finished, the yarns will move to their proper place.*

7 Weave a small piece of fabric at the end of the warp to use for testing your sewing machine tension.

Finishing

8 Remove the cloth from the loom and cut apart the napkins in the center of the scrap-yarn bands, leaving the scrap yarn in place.

9 Set your sewing machine to the smallest straight stitch. Use your test fabric to adjust your tension and practice your stitches. Machine stitch all 4 sides of your napkins ¼" (6 mm) in from the edge of the cloth.

10 Machine wash napkins on the gentle cycle. Then machine dry on low and pull out while napkins are still damp.

11 Press the cloth flat with your hands and lay flat to dry completely.

12 Using a rotary cutter and a self-healing mat, trim all 4 sides of the napkins to ¼" (6 mm) and remove any warp or weft yarns still in place.

WARP COLOR ORDER

112	56		56			☐ Yellow
64		32		32		☐ Light green
92	28	16	16	16	16	◼ Blue
108	32		32		44	☐ Yellow green
376 ends						

COMPOSITIONS AND COLORS

Weaving is an angular craft. Weavers work inside a grid, but within this grid lies a lot of patterning potential. When thinking about stripes, blocks, and plaids, I use just two simple design principles to decide how to lay them out. They are based on the beauty of mathematics and natural law. Both will help you move beyond symmetrical design.

Instead of simply dividing your warp into equal parts, consider mixing and matching different sized stripes and blocks to create a more sophisticated look. By using the Fibonacci Sequence and the Golden Mean, your stripes and blocks will always be pleasing to the eye.

Fibonacci Sequence

This numbering sequence was named after the Italian mathematician who introduced this integer series to Western European mathematics. It shows up in other natural phenomena such as branching in trees. It is easy to determine and appears harmonious to the eye.

It starts with 0+1=1, then 1+1=2, followed by 1+2=3, and so on. From that example you can see that by adding the last 2 proceeding numbers you get the next number in the sequence: 0, 1, 1, 2, 3, 5, 8, 13, 21, 34, etc.

You can use this series to determine the size of your stripes, mixing and matching according to your design, following the formula to achieve harmony. For instance, in the Twice as Nice Napkins, I used ¼" (6 mm) as my 1 and built my stripes on units of 3. So, my sequence was: 3, 5 and 8, and my stripes in the warp were ¾" [6 mm]), 1¼" (3.2 cm), and 2" (5 cm).

The Golden Mean

From a philosophical standpoint, the Golden Mean is the middle ground between two extremes. In mathematics, the Golden Mean is referred to as the golden number or ratio. It is a way of dividing a unit of measure—say, a warp width—in such a way that the smaller unit is to the larger unit as the larger unit is to the whole.

Visually, it looks like this:
To determine this ratio, you need the magic number: 1.618; 1 is the whole and .618 is the asymmetrical sweet spot that you use to figure out your design.

Say you want to create a 15" (38 cm) towel and you want to weave asymmetrical stripes.

Work this equation: 15 x .618 = 9.17. I would round up and make the larger block 9¼" (23.5 cm) just to keep the numbers tidy. A little bit here or there won't be too noticeable to the eye. I'd make the smaller strip 5¾" (14.5 cm).

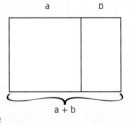

I use the Golden Mean ratio to determine my width-to-length ratio when designing a custom-sized piece for my home such as placemats, towels, and runners.

Keep in mind that fabrics such as towels and napkins are often folded, either on the table or when hanging on a bathroom rack. What appears harmonious viewed in its entirety may look a bit off when folded because the fold changes the proportions.

CHOOSING COLORS

Choosing color is either a weaver's greatest joy or biggest hassle. Reading up on color theory is helpful, but you don't have to know a lot about it to pick pleasing color combinations. I pick colors by referencing a photograph, a painting, or even an advertisement that has interesting color combinations and using them to build a color palette.

You can find an infinite number of interesting color palettes already assembled by typing, for instance "green color palette" into a search engine—you'll get dozens of results. Select the yarns that best match the image or palette and do a few yarn wraps. Wind the yarns around a 1" (2.5 cm) piece of white cardboard in the approximate proportion you would use them in the warp. Then lay the weft colors on top and see how they interact.

However, this won't give you a complete color profile of how the woven cloth will look. Color in weaving is not laid side by side, as it is in knitting, crochet, or stitching; it is typically interlaced with another yarn, so you get different optics depending on the proportion of warp to weft and fiber type. Shiny silk reflects color differently than a low-luster wool. The colors further shift during wet finishing. A quick way to test this shift is to twist your yarns together in approximate proportion as they will be in the final cloth.

Sampling is the best way to avoid surprises and to see if your ideas on paper will work off the loom. Think of sampling as risk management. I would rather take the time to weave a sample and use a little yarn than warp up my entire loom and decide that my choices aren't going to work out as I hoped.

Photographs can provide inspirational color combinations.

Luxe Linen PLACEMATS

Think outside the box when it comes to your linens. Nontraditional mixes, such as the silk-linen blend used in these placemats, make lovely table settings. Silk wears really well and is hardier than many people think. Used alone, this softly spun silk linen yarn designed for knitting creates a highly flexible textile. To create more body, use one of my favorite tricks by combining it with with a tightly spun yarn such as cottolin, pearl cotton, or rug warp. This adds stiffness and depth of color. These mats are worked in a tiny Brook's Bouquet pattern, which creates a raised texture above the nubby yarn.

PROJECT SPECS

FINISHED SIZE
Two placemats, each 12½" × 16¾" (31.5 x 43.5 cm).

WEAVE STRUCTURES
Brook's Bouquet and plain weave.

EQUIPMENT
10-dent rigid-heddle loom with a 15" (38 cm) weaving width; 3 stick shuttles.

NOTIONS
Sewing thread and needle; straight pins; tapestry needle; scrap yarn.

WARP AND WEFT SPECIFICATIONS

SETT (EPI)
10 (1 thick and 1 thin thread in each slot and hole).

WEAVING WIDTH
14½" (37 cm).

PICKS PER INCH (PPI)
9 plain weave; 6 pattern

WARP LENGTH
63" (160 cm; includes 22" [56 cm] for loom waste and take-up).

NUMBER OF ENDS
145 (290 total threads; 145 thick and 145 thin threads used together as 1 end).

RECOMMENDED WARPING METHOD
Direct.

YARNS

Warp: Silk/linen blend (1,143 yd [1,045 m]/lb): 254 yd (232 m) light green; 22/2 cottolin (3,246 yd [2,968 m]/lb): 254 yd (232 m) light green.

Shown here: Queensland Collection Savanna (66% silk/34% linen, 250 yd [229 m]/3½ oz per skein): #13 Avocado; Louet North America Organic 22/2 Cottolin (60% cotton/40% linen: 710 yd [649 m] per mini cone), #73.25051 Light Green.

Weft: Silk/linen blend: 50 yd (46 m) light green; 22/2 cottolin: 9 yd (8 m) light green.

Shown here: Queensland Collection Savanna: #13 Avocado; Louet North America Organic 22/2 Cottolin: #73.25051 Light Green.

Warping

1   Warp 2 threads together—1 thick, 1 thin—as if they were 1 end, following the project specs.

Weaving

2   Wind 1 stick shuttle with the silk/linen blend yarn, another with the cottolin, and the third with scrap yarn.

3   Weave 2" – 3" (5–7.5 cm) of scrap yarn, beating firmly to spread your warp and provide a solid foundation for your fabric (see Chapter Two).

4   Leaving a tail 6 times the width of your warp and starting in a down shed, weave 9 picks of the cottolin yarn.

5   Thread the yarn tail through a tapestry needle and, using embroidery stitch (see Chapter Ten), secure the beginning of your cloth.

6   Switch to the silk/linen blend yarn and weave ½" (1.3 cm) of plain weave, ending on a down shed and on the side of the placemat you feel most comfortable working the Brook's Bouquet pattern.

NOTE: *Brook's Bouquet is one of many popular hand-manipulated weaves. These weaves are worked in front of the heddle, and instead of passing the weft yarn straight through a shed, you wrap your shuttle around groups of the up warp ends to form little bunches or bouquets across the weft. I like to work right to left, so I ended my plain weave with my shuttle on the right side in a down shed.*

PLACEMAT 1: ALL-OVER BROOK'S BOUQUET

7   With the heddle in the up position, place your shuttle under 5 up warp ends to the left. Bring the shuttle out of the shed, pass it back over the fifth and fourth up ends to the right.

Place the shuttle back in the shed and under the next 4 up ends working to the left. You will have encased the fifth and fourth up ends for 1 pattern pick.

8   Bring the shuttle out of the shed and wrap the 2 ends to the left—the sixth and seventh ends—in the same manner by bringing the shuttle over the ends and back into the shed, passing under the next 4 ends.

Continue working in this manner.

TIP: *Lay your wrapped stitches in waves—sometimes referred to as bubbles—to allow enough slack for the weft to travel around the stitches and not cause your selvedges to draw in.*

9   When you reach the last 6 up ends, pass the shuttle under those ends and press the weft into place.

If any of the wraps seem loose, use a tapestry needle to adjust. You want to see a nice tidy X formed by the wrap.

10 Weave 1 plain weave pick.

11 Continue working alternate rows of pattern and plain weave for 16½" (42 cm). End with ½" (2.5 cm) of plain weave.

12 Fasten off the thick weft and then switch to the cottolin yarn for an additional 9 picks. Secure the end with embroidery stitch.

PLACEMAT 2: BROOK'S BOUQUET BORDERS

13 Leave a 2" (5 cm) gap between placemats.
Leaving a tail 6 times the width of your warp and starting in a down shed, weave 9 picks of the cottolin yarn.

14 Thread the yarn tail through a tapestry needle and, using embroidery stitch, secure the beginning of your cloth.

15 Switch to the silk/linen blend yarn and weave 1" (2.5 cm) of plain weave, ending on a down shed and on the side of the placemat you prefer to start the Brook's Bouquet pattern.

16 Skip under 9 ends and work the all-over Brook's Bouquet pattern, alternating with plain weave, 4 times.

In Placemat 1, you weave the Brook's Bouquet Pattern over the entire project, instead of just as a border.

17 On the fifth pattern row, skip under 9 ends, work 3 pattern picks of Brook's Bouquet, then pass the shuttle under all of the up threads until you get to the last 9 up ends. Work 3 more pattern picks, then pass the shuttle under the rest of the up warp ends.

18 Weave 1 pick of plain weave.

19 Repeat Steps 17 and 18 for 13½" (34.5 cm). Repeat Step 16 to complete the Brook's Bouquet border.

20 Weave 1" (2.5 cm) of plain weave. Fasten off the thick weft, weave 9 picks of thin weft, and then secure the end with embroidery stitch.

Finishing

21 Remove the cloth from the loom. Cut the 2 mats apart and trim the fringe to ¼" (6 mm) from the embroidery stitch.

22 To keep the hemmed warp ends from resting too far above the placemat, fold the selvedges over ¼" (6 mm) and, using coordinating sewing thread, whipstitch into place (see Chapter Ten). This will provide a firm edge all around the mat.

23 Fold the warp ends twice so that the fold meets the first thick pick. Whipstitch the fold in place.

24 Machine wash the placemats on the gentle cycle, then lay flat to dry. Trim any weft tails at their base where they meet the cloth.

Campy Gamp RUNNER

A gamp is a weaving sampler that uses different color or structure blocks to play out many different possibilities. They are beloved by weavers who use them to test lots of ideas at once. Typically they are woven "tromp as writ," meaning they are woven as they were threaded both in structure and in color. The Campy Gamp Runner combines color and pattern play. You can see how warp floats, weft floats, and a combination of the two appear in various color combinations. Keep in mind that whatever is happening on the face of the cloth as you weave, the opposite is happening on the back of the fabric.

PROJECT SPECS

FINISHED SIZE
One 8¼" × 28¾" (21 x 73 cm) runner with 1" (2.5 cm) fringe on each end.

WEAVE STRUCTURE
Pick-up.

EQUIPMENT
12-dent rigid-heddle loom with a 10" (25.5 cm) weaving width; 10" (25.5 cm) pick-up stick; 5 stick shuttles.

NOTIONS
Tapestry needle; rotary cutter and self-healing cutting mat; scrap yarn.

WARP AND WEFT SPECIFICATIONS

SETT (EPI)
12.

WEAVING WIDTH
9½" (24 cm).

PICKS PER INCH (PPI)
14.

WARP LENGTH
51" (129.5 cm; includes 18" [45.5 cm] for loom waste and take-up).

NUMBER OF ENDS
113 ends.

RECOMMENDED WARPING METHOD
Direct.

YARNS

Warp: 3/2 mercerized cotton (1,260 yd [1,152 m]/lb): 12 yd (11 m) yellow, 64 yd (59 m) pink, 43 yd (39 m) each purple, lavender.

Shown here: Cotton Clouds Pearly Pearl (100% mercerized cotton (1,260 yd [1,152 m]/lb cone): #156 Daffodil, #128 Quince (pink), #93 Deep Lavender, #81 Grotto.

Weft: 3/2 mercerized cotton: 6 yd (6 m) yellow, 32 yd (29 m) pink, 66 yd (60 m) purple, 30 yd (27 m) lavender.

Shown here: Cotton Clouds Pearly Pearl: #156 Daffodil, #128 Quince, #93 Deep Lavender, #81 Grotto.

Warping

1 Warp your loom following the project specs and the Warp Color Order chart. Start and end your warp with a yellow end in a slot.

Weaving

2 Wind 4 shuttles, 1 with each color of weft yarn, and 1 with smooth scrap yarn.

3 Weave a 1" (2.5 cm) header of scrap yarn to spread your warp (see Chapter Two).

4 Place the heddle in the down position and, working behind the heddle, pick up every other slot thread, starting with the first thread—1 up/1 down. You will end on an up.

   Push the pick-up stick to the back of the loom.

5 Leaving a tail 6 times the width of your warp, weave 2 picks of yellow.

6 Change to the pink weft yarn and weave 3 repeats of weft floats, following the Weave Color and Pattern Order chart.

7 Using the yellow tail, work a row of hemstitching around 2 warp ends and 2 weft picks.

8 Work the rest of the runner following the Weave Color and Pattern Order chart. Note that between each block is a yellow weft thread in a plain weave up shed. Carry the yellow weft along the selvedges as you weave the gamp, wrapping the weft picks around it.

   Be sure to check your PPI as you work in order to maintain a consistent block size.

TIP: *The warp-float blocks have 2 fewer picks than the weft-float blocks. This allows for a differing amount of take-up and maintains the pattern. The individual warp- and weft-float boxes should measure square on the loom, and the long windowpane warp-and weft-float boxes should be twice as long as they are wide.*

9 Finish with hemstitching, using the yellow weft as you did at the beginning of the runner.

Finishing

10 Remove the cloth from the loom, leaving the fringe long.

11 Fill a bathtub with 1"–2" (2.5–5 cm) of warm water and a tablespoon of no-rinse soap, such as Soak. Handwashing is recommended to keep the fringe from fraying.

   Lay the runner in the water and let soak for 20 minutes.

12 Pull it from the water and let the majority of the water drain away from the runner. Roll it into a tube and gently press the rest of the water out with your hands. Lay flat to dry on a clean towel.

13 Using a rotary cutter and self-healing mat, trim the fringe to 1" (2.5 cm).

WEAVE COLOR AND PATTERN ORDERS

Columns: Weft floats block, Windowpane block, Warp floats block, Plain weave

17 Lavender (number indicates picks per block)
37 Purple (number indicates picks per block)
17 Pink (number indicates picks per block)
① Yellow (number indicates number of picks)

WARP COLOR ORDER

30				15		15			▨ Lavender
30		15					15		■ Purple
45	15			15			15		▥ Pink
8	1	1	1	1	1	1	1	1	□ Yellow

113 ends

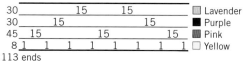

Note: This is a slot thread in beginning and end.

CAMPY GAMP PATTERN

The Campy Gamp Runner is woven by alternating blocks of warp floats, weft floats, and a combination of warp and weft floats. The pattern for each block is as follows:

Weft Float
(15 picks per block)

1   *Down.

2   Up and pick-up stick.

3   Down.

4   Up*.

   Repeat *-* 3 times for each block, then:

1   Down.

2   Up and pick-up stick.

3   Down.

Warp Floats
(17 picks per block)

1   *Down.

2   Up.

3   Pick-up stick.

4   Up*.

   Repeat *-* 4 times for each block, then:

   Down.

Windowpane:
warp and weft floats
(37 picks per block)

1   *Pick-up stick.

2   Up.

3   Down.

4   Up and pick-up stick.

5   Down.

6   Up*.

   Repeat *-* 6 times for each block, then:

   Pick-up stick.

Go Your Own Way RUNNER

This cloth was created by reverse engineering a commercial towel with a nifty little border. The design was inspired by the inlay work of one of my weaving heroes, Annie Albers. Here, the yarn sits on top of the work instead of in it, a technique popularized by another weaving innovator, Theo Moorman. By threading a thick and thin pick in each slot and hole and using a pick-up stick to pick up every slotted thin pick, you can weave a supplementary weft that sits on the cloth, in Theo Moorman style, instead of in the cloth like a traditional supplementary warp.

PROJECT SPECS

FINISHED SIZE
One 9¼" × 34¼" (23.5 cm x 87 cm) runner.

WEAVE STRUCTURE
Plain weave with inlay.

EQUIPMENT
10-dent rigid-heddle loom with a 10" (25.5 cm) weaving width; two 12"–14" (30.5–35.5 cm) stick shuttles; two 4"–6" (10–15 cm) shuttles; 14" (35.5 cm) or larger pick-up stick.

NOTIONS
Sewing thread and needle; straight pins; tapestry needle; scrap yarn; 10" x 35" (25.5 x 89 cm) strip of craft paper and colored pens or pencils (optional).

WARP AND WEFT SPECIFICATIONS

SETT (EPI)
10 (1 thick and 1 thin thread in each slot and hole).

WEAVING WIDTH
10" (25.5 cm).

PICKS PER INCH (PPI)
11.

WARP LENGTH
56" (143 cm; includes 16" [40.5 cm] for loom waste and take-up).

NUMBER OF WARP ENDS
100 (100 thick and 100 thin threads used together as 1 end).

RECOMMENDED WARPING METHOD
Direct.

YARNS

Warp: 4-ply worsted weight cotton/linen blend (1,001 yd [915 m]/lb): 156 yd (143 m) navy; 22/2 cottolin (3,246 yd [2,968 m]/lb): 156 yd (143 m) blue green.

Shown here: Rowan Creative Linen (50% cotton/50% linen, 219 yd [200 m]/ 3½ oz per skein): #635 Stormy; Louet North America Organic 22/2 Cottolin (60% cotton/40% linen, 710 yd [649 m] 3½ oz cone): #73-25034 Forest Green.

Ground weft: 4-ply worsted weight cotton: 126 yd (115 m) navy; 22/2 cottolin: 62 yd (57 m) blue green.

Shown here: Rowan Creative Linen: #635 Stormy; Louet North America Organic 22/2 Cottolin: #73-25034 Forest Green.

Supplementary weft: 4-ply worsted weight cotton/linen blend: 4 yd (4 m) yellow; 2-ply novelty cotton in a variegated colorway: 4 yd (4 m).

Shown here: Rowan Creative Line: #647 Mustard; Seedling by Classic Elite (100% organic cotton, 110 yd [100 m]/1.75 oz skein): #4528 Tahiti.

Warping

1   Warp 2 ends together—1 thick and 1 thin—as if they were 1 yarn, following the project specs and using the direct method.

Weaving

NOTE: *All thin picks are woven in a down shed, all thick picks are woven in an up shed, and the supplementary weft is woven in the pick-up stick shed. Vertical lines are formed by passing the shuttle from the front to the back of the cloth as you weave, going over the thin picks and under the thick picks. The horizontal lines are formed by placing the supplementary weft under your desired number of ends in a pick-up shed.*

2   Wind 1 of the longer shuttles with the thick navy weft yarn and the other with the thin blue-green weft yarn. Wind 1 shorter shuttle with the supplementary yellow weft yarn and the other shorter shuttle with the variegated supplementary weft yarn.

3   Weave 2"–3" (5–7.5 cm) of scrap yarn firmly to spread your warp and provide a solid foundation for your fabric (see Chapter Two).

4   Starting with the thin green weft, leave a tail 6 times the width of your warp and weave 25 picks, ending on a down shed.

5   Thread the yarn tail through a tapestry needle and use embroidery stitch (see Chapter Ten) to secure the beginning of your cloth.

     Keeping the thin green shuttle active, add in the thick navy weft. Weave ¾" (2 cm), alternating thick and thin weft yarns and ending with a thin pick on a down shed.

TIP: *I use the ply-splitting technique to decrease bulk when adding each new yarn (see Chapter Two).*

ADD INLAY WEFT YARNS

6   Place the heddle in the down position and, using a pick-up stick, pick up all the up thin ends in the slots behind the heddle.

NOTE: *The inlay may be designed on the loom, or you may wish to design a cartoon ahead of time using craft paper and colored pens or pencils.*

     Place the heddle in neutral and turn the pick-up stick on its edge. This lifts just those thin ends that are threaded in a slot above the warp.

7   Determine where you want your first supplementary weft to be, and, using 1 or 2 of the short shuttles, place the supplementary weft yarn or yarns under your desired number of ends. Use the ply-splitting technique (see Chapter Two) to decrease the visibility of the join. This forms the first horizontal line of inlay.

8   Press the yarns into place so that they slide over the thin pick. Pass each supplementary shuttle to the back of the cloth 1 thread grouping over from where you exited the thin-pick shed. This makes for a tidier turn than if you were turning on a thick pick.

TIP: *You are now managing 4 shuttles. Because you need to bring the shuttle to the back of the cloth regularly, it may be useful to work on a stand so that you can place the supplementary shuttles on your lap as you work.*

9   Place the heddle in the up position and weave a thick pick. Bring the supplementary shuttles back up through the cloth at the same position you passed it to the back side so that your other wefts go under the thick pick. This is the beginning of the vertical row of inlay.

10   Weave 1 thin pick.

     At this point, you have a choice: You can either continue the vertical line by passing the shuttle to the back of the cloth or place the heddle in neutral, engage the pick-up stick, and lay in a horizontal row.

11 Continue working, either designing your unique inlay pattern on the loom or following your paper-cartoon. When the body of the runner measures 35" (89 cm) on the loom, end the inlay pattern using the ply-splitting method to reduce the join's bulk.

12 Use the 2 ground wefts to weave ¾" of plain weave as you did before. Fasten off the thick weft and finish the runner with 15 picks of the thin weft and embroidery stitch.

Finishing

13 Remove the cloth from the loom. Trim the fringe to ¼" (6 mm) from the embroidery stitching.

14 Fold the warp ends over ½" (1.3 cm), then fold again so that the fold meets the first thick pick and pin into place. Press, then whipstitch (see Chapter Ten) to secure.

15 Machine wash the runner on the gentle cycle. Lay flat to dry. Trim any weft tails at their base where they meet the cloth.

MAKING A CARTOON

You can either design your inlay-style pattern as you go on the loom or create a cartoon. Cartoons are used regularly in tapestry weaving. The weaver sketches out her design on paper, then places it behind the loom to follow as she weaves. Most tapestry weavers work on a vertical loom, which makes this easier to do. Still, rigid-heddle-loom weavers can use cartoons, too.

As you weave on a rigid-heddle loom, the cloth rolls around the cloth beam and you are unable to see your work as a whole. For this reason, I sketched out my lines on a to-scale paper cartoon so I could get a sense of the design before starting and could follow it as a guide while I worked.

To make a cartoon, cut a piece of craft paper the size of your work; in the case of the Go Your Own Way Runner, make it 10" x 35" (25.5 x 89 cm). Mark the sides of the paper with hashmarks every 1" (2.5 cm) so you can get a sense of scale. Use 2 different-colored pens or pencils to rough out your design, remembering that all inlay lines must be either vertical or horizontal or stair-stepped diagonals. Place the cartoon on a table or floor near the loom and use it as a guide as you weave.

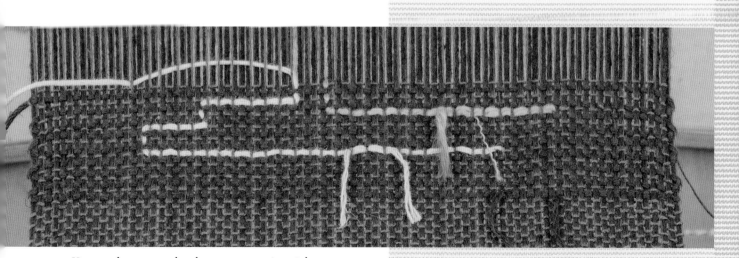

Use supplementary shuttles to create unique inlay patterns.

CHAPTER SIX

THE LIVING ROOM

Wool lovers rejoice! Living spaces are the perfect place for cozy throws and chubby pillows that invite you to curl up with a good book and a favorite beverage and relax. Handwoven textiles brighten up any spot—tuck table squares under a favorite lamp, use them to highlight a piece of pottery, or declare a TV remote station. Beautiful and functional, rugs are not just for the floor. Small table-top rugs add texture to a room and protect your tables from the accidentally knocked-over cup of tea or prevent your pens from rolling away.

Hudson Bay INSPIRED THROW

A big, cozy throw such as this one is absolutely within reach of a rigid-heddle-loom weaver, both figuratively and literally. A second heddle allows you to weave cloth twice the width of your loom. Inspired by the iconic Hudson Bay point blankets with their bold stripes, this version uses naturally colored wool and incorporates the small lines indicating the size of the blanket on a traditional Hudson Bay point blanket.

PROJECT SPECS

FINISHED SIZE
One 37¾" x 69" (96 x 175 cm) throw with 6" (15 cm) fringe.

WEAVE STRUCTURE
Double-width doubleweave.

EQUIPMENT
Rigid-heddle loom with a 24" (61 cm) weaving width; two 5-dent rigid heddles; 4 stick shuttles; two 26" (66 cm) pick-up sticks.

NOTIONS
Scrap yarn.

WARP AND WEFT SPECIFICATIONS

SETT (EPI)
10 (5 for each layer).

WEAVING WIDTH
24" (61 cm).

PICKS PER INCH (PPI)
6.

WARP LENGTH
3 yd (2.75 m; includes 29" [73.5 cm] for loom waste and take-up; loom waste includes fringe).

NUMBER OF WARP ENDS
240.

RECOMMENDED WARPING METHOD
Indirect or direct 2 heddle.

YARNS

Warp: 2-ply bulky wool (874 yd [799 m]/lb): 720 yd (658 m) white.

Shown here: Cascade Yarns Ecological Wool (100% wool, 478 yd [437m]/8¾ oz skein): #8014 Vanilla.

Weft: 2-ply bulky wool: 562 yd (514 m) white; 66 yd (60 m) each medium brown, dark brown.

Shown here: Cascade Yarns Ecological Wool: #8014 Vanilla, #8063 Latte, #8087 Chocolate.

Warping

1. Warp your loom using either the direct or indirect 2-heddle warping method, following the project specs. (See Chapter Nine for tips on 2-heddle warping and warping long, wide warps and Mesaland Doubleweave Pillow Cover for more information on how doubleweave works.)

Weaving

2. Wind 1 shuttle with each of the 3 color weft yarns and a fourth shuttle with smooth scrap yarn.

3. Weave a 1"–2" (2.5–5 cm) header of scrap yarn to spread your warp (see Chapter Two).

   Before starting your throw, ensure that you have 8" (20.5 cm) of warp either unwoven or woven with scrap yarn that can be used for fringe.

   Then weave 1" (2.5 cm) with scrap yarn in the pattern to keep the weft in place when you cut the project from the loop and unfold the blanket.

PLACE PICK-UP STICKS

Pick-Up Stick A

4. Place both heddles in the down position. Working behind the heddles and starting with the first up end, pick up every other warp end.

WEAVE COLOR ORDER

Medium brown / Dark brown / White

		8¼" (21 cm)
3¾"		(9.5 cm)
	3¾"	(9.5 cm)
3¾"		(9.5 cm)
		1" (2.5 cm)
	2 short dark brown stripes using clasped weft	
		1" (2.5 cm)
	2 short dark brown stripes using clasped weft	
		37" (94 cm)
3¾"		(9.5 cm)
	3¾"	(9.5 cm)
3¾"		(9.5 cm)
		8¼" (21 cm)

Pick-Up Stick B

5. Place both heddles in the up position. Slide pick-up stick A toward the heddles so that it touches heddle 2. Place pick-up stick B behind the heddles in the lowest shed.

WEAVE ONE PATTERN REPEAT

6. Starting on the right side, engage pick-up stick B by placing both heddles in neutral and tipping the pick-up stick on its edge. Using the white weft and leaving a 6" (15 cm) tail, weave the first pick (lower layer).

7. Lay pick-up stick B flat and push it to the back of the loom. Place heddle 2 in the up position and weave the second pick (upper layer).

8. With the heddles in neutral, engage pick-up stick A and weave a third pick (upper layer).

9. Place heddle 1 in the down position. For this 1 pick, tuck the weft tail into the shed to secure it (lower layer).

10. Repeat Steps 6–9 to weave this 4-step sequence for another 1"–2" (2.5 - 5 cm).

CHECK YOUR WORK

11. Place heddle 2 in the up position. Pull heddle 1 toward the back of that heddle, lifting the upper layer of warp threads above the lower layer.

    Two selvedge edges should be on the right side and a fold on the left where the 2 layers are connected.

NOTE: *I recommend starting on the right, if you start on the left, there may be a double end in the fold. If so, cut the yarn threaded through the outer most edge away to maintain the over/under weaving order.*

12. Continue weaving following the Weave Color Order chart.

WEAVE THE SHORT STRIPES

13. With heddle 2 in the up position, weave 1 pick of the working white weft yarn, stopping 4" (10 cm) short of the right selvedge edge. Bring the shuttle out of the shed. Rest it on the weaving.

14 Take the shuttle with the dark brown weft yarn into the same shed from the right, leaving a 4" (10 cm) tail. Bring it out of the shed at the same point where the white weft exited. Lay it on the cloth.

15 Clasp the 2 wefts by bringing the dark brown weft yarn around the white weft yarn.

16 Change the shed to the other upper shed by engaging pick-up stick A. Place the white warp in the shed, moving it to the left, and the dark brown weft into the shed, moving it to the right.

17 Weave 1" (2.5 cm) of white weft yarn, carrying the dark brown weft yarn up the selvedge.

18 Weave a second short brown stripe. Use the ply-splitting technique (see Chapter Two) to end the dark brown weft yarn and then finish weaving the blanket following the Weave Color Order chart.

Depending on your loom style, toward the end of weaving the throw, you may come close to filling your front beam and the cloth may start pushing on your shed, causing your shed height to decrease, making it harder for you to get a clean shed. If this happens, advance your warp every 1" (2.5 cm).

19 Weave 3" (7.5 cm) of scrap yarn to keep the weft secure during finishing.

Finishing

20 Remove the cloth from the loom, leaving at least 8" (20 cm) of warp for fringe on each end. Trim any tails to 2" (5 cm).

You may have floats on the bottom layer. You can't see the bottom layer as you work, and it is very easy to accidentally miss the over/under configuration, particularly with wools that may stick together. Check the cloth for any skips and fix before washing (see Chapter Ten).

21 Use overhand knots to tie groups of 4 warp threads snugged up to the end of the throw (see Chapter Ten). Trim the fringe to 6" (15.2 cm) or your desired length. Trim any tails flush with the cloth.

22 This is a case of knowing thy washing machine. You can wash this throw on the handwash or delicate cycle of your machine, but the most conservative way of washing is by hand. The danger to the cloth is the agitator, which can snag the fringe and skew the fabric.

If you need to, handwash by filling a bathtub with lukewarm water. Add either a ¼ cup mild or no-rinse detergent. Place the cloth in the bathtub and swish about generously. Allow the fabric to soak for 20 minutes. Drain and rinse.

23 Holding the throw over the tub for a minute or two, let the excess water flow out, then gently press the cloth with your hands to get out any excess water. Drape clean towels over a drying rack and lay the throw on them to dry.

DOUBLE-WIDTH DOUBLEWEAVE PATTERN

Double-width doubleweave is worked over 4 picks:

1   Pick-up stick B (lower layer).
2   Heddle 2 up (upper layer).
3   Pick-up stick A (upper layer).
4   Heddle 1 down (lower layer.)

Tweed and Twill PILLOW COVER

An iconic fabric of the Irish and British countryside, tweed is one of the most recognizable woven fabrics and is beloved by weavers around the world. Classic tweed is woolen fabric woven in plain weave or twill. This oversized tweed pillow is made from a worsted-spun Romney longwool yarn that will wear for generations. It gives the fabric a classic look, and the mossy colors are reminiscent of the hills of the British Isles. The pillow cover is reversible and can easily be sized up or down to accommodate the width of your loom or your preferred pillow size.

PROJECT SPECS

FINISHED SIZE
One pillow cover 21½" x 21½" (54.5 x 54.5 cm) with an 8" (20.5 cm) closure flap and 5" (12.5 cm) staggered bound warp fringe.

WEAVE STRUCTURE
1/3 Twill.

EQUIPMENT
Rigid-heddle loom with a 23" (58.5 cm) weaving width; two 5-dent rigid heddles; 2 stick shuttles; two 26" (66 cm) pick-up sticks; 26" (66 cm) heddle rod; 57 string heddles.

NOTIONS
Sewing thread and needle; straight pins; 20" x 20" (51 x 51 cm) pillow form; scrap yarn; 3 large snaps (optional).

WARP AND WEFT SPECIFICATIONS

SETT (EPI)
10.

WEAVING WIDTH
22¾" (58 cm).

PICKS PER INCH (PPI)
7.

WARP LENGTH
82" (208 cm; includes 24" [61 cm] for loom waste and take-up; loom waste includes fringe).

NUMBER OF WARP ENDS
228.

RECOMMENDED WARPING METHOD
Indirect or direct 2-heddle.

YARNS

Warp: 2-ply bulky-weight wool, (800 yd [732 m]/lb): 520 yd (475 m) green.

Shown here: Fancy TigerCrafts Heirloom Romney (100% wool, 200 yd [183 m]/4 oz skein): Nettles.

Weft: 2-ply bulky-weight wool: 285 yd [261 m]) yellow.

Shown here: Fancy Tiger Crafts Heirloom Romney: Mullein.

Finishing: 22/2 cottolin (2,900 yd [2,652 m]/lb): 20 yd (18 m) yellow.

Shown here: Louet North America Organic 22/2 Cottolin (60% cotton/40% linen; 710 yd [649 m] /3½ oz mini cone): Very Light Yellow.

Warping

1. Warp your loom using a direct or indirect 2-heddle warping method, following the project specs. (See Chapter Nine for tips on 2-heddle warping and warping long, wide warps.)

TIP: *Good tension is important for getting a clean shed with sticky wools such as Romney, so take care to pack your beam well and keep tight tension on the warp as you work.*

Weaving

2. Wind 1 shuttle with the weft yarn and 1 shuttle with scrap yarn.

3. Weave a 1"–2" (2.5–5 cm) header of smooth scrap yarn to spread your warp (see Chapter Two).

PLACE PICK-UP STICK

4. Place both heddles in the down position. Working behind the heddles, pick 1 up/1 down across the width of the warp. Slide the pick-up stick to the back of the loom.

PLACE HEDDLE ROD

5. Place both heddles in the down position. Working from the back, pick 1 down/1 up across the width of the warp in the opposite configuration as you picked up on the first pick-up stick in Step 4.

6. Place both heddles in neutral, tip the pick-up stick on its edge, and place each up end on a heddle rod.

7. Using the yellow weft yarn and leaving a tail 6 times the width of the fabric, weave 3" (7.5 cm) following the 1/3 twill pattern sequence.

   Watch for the diagonal green lines of warp that will form as you weave. If you see a break in the line, you have probably missed a step in the sequence and must either unweave back to that step or clip out the picks of weaving that came after that step.

8. Work a row of embroidery stitch (see Chapter Ten) to secure the beginning of the work.

9. Continue weaving for a total of 58" (147.5 cm).

TIPS: *It is important that you maintain your weft angle and advance often as you do so to keep the selvedge even and to prevent crowding at the connected selvedge.*

This fabric is slightly warp dominant, which will show more on the back than it will on the face of the cloth. Weave with a light beat, maintaining a consistent number of picks per 1" (2.5 cm).

Keep an eye on the selvedge as you work. Because of the nature of twill, you will have a float traveling over 3 ends at the selvedge in every group of 4 picks. Catch this selvedge as you work by manually breaking the structure and picking up the selvedge thread.

10. Weave a few picks with scrap yarn to keep the weft secure during finishing.

Finishing

11 Remove the cloth from the loom. Trim any tails to 2" (5 cm). Check the cloth for any skips and fix before washing (see Chapter Ten).

12 Fold the end over ½" (1.3 cm) and secure with embroidery stitch. Fold again 2" (5 cm) to encase the fringe. Pin the seam to secure for stitching. Using coordinating sewing thread, whipstitch the fold in place (see Chapter Ten).

13 For the decorative fringe on the flap, work 3 rows of staggered bound warp with the 22/2 yellow cottolin (see Chapter Ten). The first row will have 19 groups of 12 warp ends.

14 With the hemmed tab at the bottom, fold the fabric over at 21" (53.5 cm) to form a square pocket with an 8" flap.

   Rather than attempting to seamlessly join the sides of the pillow, highlight them using the Eskimo join (Chapter Ten) and the yellow weft yarn.

15 Handwash the pillow cover by filling a bathtub with lukewarm water. Add ¼ cup mild or no-rinse detergent. Place the cover in the bathtub and swish vigorously. Allow the fabric to soak for 20 minutes. Drain and rinse if necessary.

   Briefly holding the pillow cover over the tub, let the excess water flow out, then roll gently. Press the cloth with your hands to get out any excess water. Air-dry flat on a clean towel.

16 Trim the fringe to 2½" (6.5 cm) or your desired length. Trim any tails flush with the cloth.

17 Insert a pillow form. If desired, space 3 snaps evenly under the flap near the fringe edge to secure it to the body of the pillow cover.

1/3 TWILL PATTERN

Work 1/3 twill over 4 picks as follows:

1 Heddle 1 up.
2 Pick-up stick.
3 Heddle 2 up.
4 Heddle rod.

WHAT IS A TWILL?

In its simplest form, a twill is a structure in which each weft pick and warp end passes over or under more than one thread. Each successive pick is worked in the same interlacement offset by one warp thread. This is what creates the easily recognizable, strong diagonal pattern in a twill. This is either continuous or, sometimes, broken to gain different effects.

Twill fabrics are reversible. When worked in two colors, such as in this pillow cover, whichever yarn color is the dominant color on the front will be the secondary color on the back. There are many, many kinds of twill, a few of which are used in this book's patterns.

The 1/3 twill used to weave the Tweed and Twill Pillow Cover is what most folks think of when they think "twill." The weft passes under one warp and over three wefts, which creates a strong diagonal line.

The Bird's Eye Twill used in the Fresh Baked Bread Cloth is a mixed twill. It mixes the float arrangement, moving between going over three wefts to going under three wefts.

The Point Twill used in the Twill Be Done Runner also has a strong diagonal line. But the warp and weft floats are worked over two ends, and the twill is worked in one direction and then is worked in the opposite direction forming a point.

The Advancing Twill, also used in the Twill Be Done Runner, gets into some of the fancier twills that combine both the plain and mixed twills into some really incredible structures.

Bejeweled **TABLE SQUARE**

Handpainted yarns make eye-catching color-and-weave patterns, such as this log cabin, even more dazzling. The log cabin pattern is a favorite of many weavers because it creates the illusion of a woven fabric within a woven fabric. Using a handpainted yarn as the dark end and a solid color as the light end increases the richness of the optical illusion. Table squares make a perfect focal point on a side table.

PROJECT SPECS

FINISHED SIZE
One 13" x 12½" (33 x 31.5 cm) table square.

WEAVE STRUCTURE
Log Cabin.

EQUIPMENT
12-dent rigid-heddle loom with a 14" (35.5 cm) weaving width; 4 stick shuttles.

NOTIONS
Sewing thread and needle; liquid seam sealer such as Fray Check; scrap yarn.

WARP AND WEFT SPECIFICATIONS

SETT (EPI)
12.

WEAVING WIDTH
14" (35.5 cm).

PICKS PER INCH (PPI)
12.

WARP LENGTH
36" (91 cm; includes 20" [50.8 cm] for loom waste and take-up).

NUMBER OF WARP ENDS
168.

RECOMMENDED WARPING METHOD
Indirect or direct.

YARNS

Warp: 4-pl sportweightht wet-spun linen (1,300 yd [1,189 m]/lb): 84 yd (77 m) each cream, handpainted multicolored.

Shown here: Louet Euroflax Sport (100% wet-spun linen, 270 yd [247 m]/3½ oz skein): #18.2014 Champagne; Alpine(hand dyed by Prism Yarns).

Weft: 4-ply sportweight wet-spun linen: 36 yd (33 m) each cream, handpainted multicolored; sewing thread, 10 yd (9 m).

Shown here: Louet Euroflax Sport: #18.2014 Champagne, Alpine (hand-dyed by Prism Yarns).

Warping

1   Warp your loom, following the project specs and the Warp Color Order chart, using either the direct or indirect method.

Weaving

2   Wind 1 shuttle with handpainted weft yarn, 1 shuttle with cream weft yarn, 1 shuttle with the coordinating sewing thread, and 1 shuttle with scrap yarn.

3   Weave a 1" (2.5 cm) header of scrap yarn to spread your warp (see Chapter Two).

4   Leaving a 6" (15.2 cm) tail, weave 1" (2.5 cm) with sewing thread. This will make your seams almost flat so that they don't rise above the cloth when laid flat. Tuck in the tail with the second pick. Secure the ends with liquid seam sealer.

5   Continue weaving the cloth in the same order as it was threaded, following the Weave Color Order chart. As you weave, wrap the working end around the nonworking end to create a tidy edge.

6   End with 1" (2.5 cm) sewing thread and secure with liquid seam sealer.

Finishing

7   Remove the cloth from the loom. Trim the warp to ¼" (6 mm) from the sealed ends.

8   Fold the end over ¼" (6 mm) and then fold again at the transition between the sewing thread and linen. Pin the seam to secure for stitching and press. Use coordinating sewing thread to whip-stitch the fold in place (see Chapter Ten).

9   Machine wash the project on the gentle cycle in warm water with a regular detergent. Include a terry-cloth towel in the washing machine with the mat to help provide some additional agitation and protect it from the agitator. Lay flat to dry.

10   Trim any remaining tails flush with the cloth.

WARP COLOR ORDER

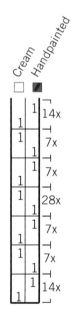

	Cream	Handpainted	
	□	◪	
		1	14x
	1		
	1		7x
		1	
		1	7x
	1		
	1		28x
		1	
		1	7x
	1		
	1		7x
		1	
		1	14x
	1		

WEAVE COLOR ORDER

	14x	7x	7x	28x	7x	7x	14x	
84	1		1 1		1 1		1 1	□ Cream
84	1 1		1 1		1 1		1	◪ Handpainted

168 ends

WARPING A LOG CABIN PATTERN

Log cabin is one of many color-and-weave structures that use light and dark ends to create a seemingly complex structure. The optics of light and dark create the pattern.

To wind complicated color orders, such as those used in the Bejeweled Table Square, I used a warping board because I find it easier to wind 2 warps, 1 of each color, and then thread each color separately. (See Chapter Nine for tips on how to pick the best warping method.)

If you decide to use the direct warping method, you need to alternate the order of your light and dark end groupings according to the pattern. In this case, you would warp the slots first as shown in the Initial Threading of Slots for Log Cabin chart.

When you thread the holes, you will move the threads into their proper position. However, instead of consistently working in one direction, you will need to change the direction each time the color order changes.

Unlike what you may be used to, you will change the threading order of the slots as well as threading the holes.

Starting on the left, thread both the slots and holes as follows; you will always work the light ends to the right, but you will change the working order of the dark ends from right to left:

1   Move dark ends into the slots; move light ends into the holes working right for 28 ends.

2   Move dark ends into the holes working left; move light ends into the slots working right for 14 ends.

3   Move dark ends into the slots; move light ends into the holes working right for 14 ends.

4   Move dark ends into the holes working left; move light ends into the slots working right for 56 ends.

5   Move dark ends into the slots; move light ends into the holes working right for 14 ends.

6   Move dark ends into the holes working left; move light ends into the slots working right for 14 ends.

7   Move dark ends into the slots; move light ends into the holes working right for 28 ends.

This will be way more confusing to your head than it will be to your hands! You can spot-check your work by looking at the yarns threaded in the holes. You should see the colors in the holes change as the color order changes. Refer to the the Final Threading Order for Log Cabin chart.

Initial Threading of Slots for Log Cabin

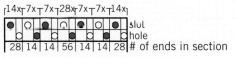

⊘ Light ends
● Dark ends

Final Threading Order for Log Cabin

Oversized MUG RUGS

Coasters just don't cut it compared to these oversized mug rugs.
I have one in every room of my home. They provide a designated place
to set my favorite beverage with room left over for my cell phone,
remote, threading needle, keys, jewelry, or whatever else needs a
special spot to lay. Self-striping sock, space-dyed, or hand-dyed
gradient yarns offer loads of patterning power with none of the work.
This project gives the appearance of a small rug.

PROJECT SPECS

FINISHED SIZE
Three mug rugs, each 7½" x 8¼"
(19 x 21 cm).

WEAVE STRUCTURE
Weft-faced plain weave.

EQUIPMENT
8-dent rigid-heddle loom with an 8"
(20.5 cm) weaving width; 2 stick
shuttles; tapestry beater.

NOTIONS
Rotary cutter and self-healing mat;
scrap yarn.

WARP AND WEFT SPECIFICATIONS

SETT (EPI)
8.

WEAVING WIDTH
8" (20.5 cm).

PICKS PER INCH (PPI)
50.

WARP LENGTH
65" (183 cm; includes 38" [96.5
cm] for loom waste, take-up, and
interstitial fringe).

NUMBER OF ENDS
64.

RECOMMENDED WARPING METHOD
Direct.

YARNS

Warp: 8/4 cotton carpet warp
(1,600 yd [1,463 m]/lb): 116 yd
(106 m) light green.

Shown here: Cotton Clouds Rug
Warp (100% unmercerized cotton;
800 yd [731m]/8 oz cone): #45
Aqua Green.

Weft: Self-striping sock, space-
dyed, or gradient wool or wool blend
(about 2,000 yd [1,828m]/lb): 110
yd (100 m) for each colorway.

Shown here: Berroco Sox (75%
superwash wool/25% nylon), 440 yd
[402 m]/3½ oz ball): #1490
Stewart; Crystal Palace Mini Mochi
(80% merino wool/20% nylon,
195 yd [178 m]/1¾ oz ball): #124
Leaves & Sprouts; Lorna's Laces
Shepherd Sport (100% superwash,
200 yd [183 m]/2 oz ball)
Northbrook.

Warping

1   Warp your loom following the project specs and using the direct method.

Weaving

2   Wind 2 shuttles, 1 with the pattern weft yarn and the other with a generous amount of scrap yarn.

TIP: *Wind the entire weft yardage 110 yd (100 m) so that the color pattern of the yarn stays intact in your weaving. If you do run short, wind off another ball from your original ball and then rewind the same yarn onto your shuttle so that the end of the yarn that came off the ball first comes off the shuttle first.*

3   Weave a 1" (2.5 cm) header of scrap yarn to spread your warp (see Chapter Two).

4   Leaving a 4" (10 cm) tail, weave 1 pick. Open a second shed and tuck the tail into this shed 2" (5 cm). Allow the rest of the tail to exit the warp.

5   Continue weaving, packing the weft firmly with the rigid heddle as you weave. Stop every 1" (2.5 cm) with the heddle in the position for the next shed—if you just wove an up shed, place the heddle in the down position or vice versa.

     Use a tapestry beater to firmly pack the weft (see Chapter Two). You will likely compress the warp to half its height. As you weave, maintain a weft angle that neither pulls in at the edges nor leaves loops.

6   Once you have woven 8½" (21.5 cm), end each rug with at least 1" (2.5 cm) of scrap yarn.

7   Leave 10" (25.5 cm) or more between each rug to allow plenty of fringe length for knotting, braiding, or weaving your selvedges, if you choose.

8   Repeat Steps 4–7 twice more to weave 2 more mug rugs.

Finishing

9   Remove the cloth from the loom. Cut the mug rugs apart, leaving an equal amount of fringe for each one.

10   Work the fringe in the finishing of your choice (see Chapter Ten). Shown below, on the top rug, I've worked a traditional woven edge rug finish. You can work side to side as I did here, or, if you prefer a braid at each corner, work from the middle out. On the second rug, I used a 4-stranded flat braid so that the fringe lays flat. I finished the third rug using staggered knots.

11   Using a rotary cutter and self-healing mat, trim fringe to desired length after finishing. Then trim any tails flush with the cloth.

12   It is not necessary to wet-finish these rugs. After a bit of use, though, you may want to freshen them up.

     Soak them in a bowl filled with lukewarm water and a tablespoon of mild detergent for 20 minutes. Remove projects, refill basin with clean water, and gently swish the rug about to rinse. Remove the rug and roll it in a towel to press out excess water. Lay flat to dry.

Market Day MIXED-WARP PILLOW

Recycled sari silk woven in a mixed warp creates a riot of color and textures reminiscent of an Indian market. Mixed warps are also a great way to use up little bits of yarn, particularly textured mohair or bouclé. To get a clean shed with sticky yarns, you need to either use them in a very open sett or intermingle them with a smoother yarn.

PROJECT SPECS

FINISHED SIZE
One 17" x 14½" (43 x 37 cm) pillow cover.

WEAVE STRUCTURE
Plain weave.

EQUIPMENT
8-dent rigid-heddle loom with a 17" (43 cm) weaving width; 2 stick shuttles.

NOTIONS
Tapestry needle; sewing thread and needle; 16" x 12" (40.5 x 30.5 cm) pillow form; scrap yarn.

WARP AND WEFT SPECIFICATIONS

SETT (EPI)
8.

WEAVING WIDTH
16¼" (41.5 cm).

PICKS PER INCH (PPI)
8.

WARP LENGTH
62" (157.5 cm; includes 22" [55.9 cm] for loomwaste and take-up).

NUMBER OF WARP ENDS
127.

RECOMMENDED WARPING METHOD
Indirect.

YARNS

Warp: Sportweight wool singles (1,325 yd [1,211 m]/lb): 43 yd (39 m) yellow; mohair bouclé (914 yd [836 m]/lb): 43 yd (39 m) blue; 3-ply worsted-weight wool (1,682 yd [1,538 m]/lb): 43 yd (39 m) purple; worsted-weight mercerized cotton (987 yd [902 m]/lb): 45 yd (41 m) rose; brushed mohair (1,175 yd [1,073 m]/lb): 45 yd (41 m) green.

Shown here: Lanaloft Spor0; 145 yd [132 m]/1¾ oz skein): #L57 Lemon Pound Cake; Be Sweet Mohair Bouclé (100% baby mohair, 100 yd [91 m]/1¾ oz ball): #19a DarkDenim; Brown Sheep Nature SpunSport (100% wool, 184 yd [168 m]/1¾ oz ball): #207 Alpine Violet; Tahki-Stacy Charles Cotton Classic (108 yd [99 m]/1¾ oz skein) #3415 Raspberry; Halcyon Yarn Victorian Brushed Mohair (74% mohair/16% wool/10% nylon; 1,025 yd [937 m]/14 oz skein): #1320 Green.

Weft: Worsted-weight recycled silk (411 yd [376 m]/lb): 160 yd (146 m) jewel tones.

Shown here: Darn Good Yarn Premium Sari Silk Handspun Yarn (100% recycled silk); 90 yd [75 m]/3½ oz skein: colors will vary.

Seaming: Laceweight unmercerized cotton (1,600 yd [1,463 m]/lb): 2 yd (1.8 m) rose; 1" (2.5 cm wide silk ribbon: 1 yd (1 m) orange.

Shown here: Darn Good Yarn Sari Silk Ribbon (100 % recycled silk) 50 yd (46 m)/skein, colors will vary.

Warping

1 Warp the loom following the project specs and the Warp Color Order chart using the indirect method.

TIP: *Good, tight tension will help you get a clean shed. If warping from your stash, be sure that you place smooth yarns between sticky yarns. Keep the sticky yarns to one or two varieties in the warp. If you find it difficult to get a good shed, insert a pick-up stick inside and in front of the loom and then tip it on its edge to clear the shed. Lightly spraying the warp with leave-in hair conditioner or hair spray may also help.*

Weaving

2 Wind 1 shuttle with the weft yarn and 1 shuttle with smooth bulky scrap yarn that will be easy to remove from the warp.

3 Weave a 1" (2.5 cm) header of scrap yarn to spread your warp (see Chapter Two).

4 Leaving a 6" (15 cm) tail, weave 1 pick with the ground weft. Open a second shed, tuck the tail into this shed 2" (5 cm), and allow the rest of the tail to exit the warp.

5 Continue weaving for 40" (101.5 cm). Watch that you have a clean shed each time. Keep a pick-up stick handy to clear the shed, particularly when you advance the warp. The yarns are sticky enough that you don't need to secure the warp at the other end.

  You can leave a short fringe on the pillow cover, as shown in the alternate version.

Finishing

6 Remove the cloth from the loom. Trim any tails to 2" (5 cm). Remove the header.

7 Handwash the cloth by filling a bathtub or large container with a few inches of lukewarm water. Add either ⅛ cup of mild or no-rinse detergent. Allow to soak for 20 minutes, then rinse.

  Remove the fabric from the water, holding it over the tub for a minute to let the excess water flow out. Roll the fabric in a towel and press, don't wring, to remove any additional water. Dry flat on a clean towel.

8 Rub your hand back and forth across the fabric to raise the texture of the bouclé above the fabric.

9 Trim the fringe ½" (1.3 cm) from each end of the cloth and any tails flush with the cloth.

SEWING THE PILLOW COVER

10 Fold each end over ½" (1.3 cm) and then fold again to encase the raw edge. Whipstitch in place (see Chapter Ten).

11 Fold the fabric in half lengthwise. Pin in place. Stitch the side seams together using the invisible seam (see Chapter Ten), stopping at the base of the whipstitched seam. Insert the pillow form.

12 With the silk ribbon and tapestry needle, use the running stitch to sew the ends together at the base of the seams, using a stitch length of ½" (1.3 cm). Secure the end by knotting in the seam and then burying the end on the inside of the pillow.

WARP COLOR ORDER

	25x			
25	1			☐ Yellow wool single
25		1		▥ Blue bouclé
25			1	■ Purple 3-ply wool
26	1		1	▦ Rose cotton
26	1		1	▨ Green brushed mohair

127 ends

Mesaland DOUBLEWEAVE PILLOW COVER

Tubular doubleweave allows you to weave two separate layers of cloth, one right on top of the other, that are connected at the selvedges—you weave a tube right on the loom. By securing the two layers together as you start to weave and leaving the end open, you only have to sew one seam to make a pillow. This structure also gives you the opportunity to play with color. You can thread one color on the top layer and another on the bottom layer.

PROJECT SPECS

FINISHED SIZE
One 20" x 19½" (51 x 49.5 cm) pillow cover.

WEAVE STRUCTURE
Tubular doubleweave.

EQUIPMENT
Rigid-heddle loom with a 23" (58.5 cm) weaving width; two 8-dent heddles; 4 stick shuttles; sewing machine (optional).

NOTIONS
20" (51 cm) pillow insert; tapestry needle; scrap yarn; sewing thread and needle (optional); 19" (48.5 cm) zipper (optional).

WARP AND WEFT SPECIFICATIONS

SETT (EPI)
16 (8 for each layer).

WEAVING WIDTH
21¾" (55 cm).

PICKS PER INCH (PPI)
8.

WARP LENGTH
40" (101.5 cm).

NUMBER OF WARP ENDS
352.

RECOMMENDED WARPING METHOD
Indirect.

YARNS

Warp: 4-ply worsted-weight cotton/linen blend (1,001 yd [915 m]/lb): 136 yd (125 m) tan, 120 yd (110 m) cream, 136 yd (125 m) pink.

Shown here: Rowan Creative Linen (50% cotton/50% linen, 219 yd [200 m]/3½ oz skein): #621 Natural, #622 Straw, #642 Pink Mist.

Weft: 4-ply worsted-weight cotton/linen blend: tan 118 yd (108 m), pink 143 yd (131 m).

Shown here: Rowan Creative Linen; #622 Straw, #642 Pink Mist.

HOW DOUBLEWEAVE WORKS

Doubleweave allows you to weave 2 separate layers on the loom at the same time, stacked right on top of each other. This gives you the possibilities of leaving the selvedges open, connecting the 2 layers at 1 side, connecting them at both sides, interchanging the layers for color blocks, or even alternating all four—a dizzying array of options.

My favorite way to use doubleweave is to connect just 1 selvedge and weave a fabric twice the width of my loom or connect both selvedges to weave a tube for bags and pillows (photos 1 and 2).

Doubleweave can be tricky the first time you try it. Two areas I see weavers get turned around is when selecting yarns for doubleweave.

Sett

With tubular and double-width doubleweave projects, you are weaving 2 separate cloths at the same time. To do this, you need to pick a yarn that has a balanced plain-weave sett of your desired final cloth, but in practice, because you are using 2 heddles, you are warping and weaving with twice that number of ends in 1" (2.5 cm). This creates a very dense warp that is prone to sticking, particularly if you are using wool.

As a refresher, here is quick way to gauge a balanced plain-weave sett for any given yarn. Balanced plain weave is a fabric that has the same number of warp ends and weft picks in 1" (2.5 cm) of cloth. Wind a yarn around a ruler for 1" (2.5 cm) using moderate tension; you want to mimic the yarn in its relaxed state, then divide the number of wraps in half. This takes into account that you will be weaving your weft in and out of these yarns on the loom.

For example, if a yarn wraps 1" (2.5 cm) 12 times, a balanced plain-weave sett is 6. Keep in mind this is a very rough estimate. Several other factors go into selecting a sett such as yarn type, construction, and final use.

To mitigate a sticky warp, choose an open sett or a sett slightly smaller than a balanced plain-weave sett of your yarn. The wool yarn used in the Hudson Bay Inspired Throw in Chapter Six has a balanced plain-weave sett of 6. Selecting a size 5 rigid heddle means there is a bit of wiggle room on either side of the yarn.

Smooth cottons or cotton blends used in the Mesa-land Doubleweave Pillow Cover are good choices for your first doubleweave projects as they are less likely to stick than wool. I also recommend investing in larger heddles and weaving a chunky project as you are building skills because the fabric works up more quickly and it is easier to see what you are doing.

Doubleweave layers woven independent of one another.

Doubleweave layers joined at the selvedge.

Charging Pick-Up Sticks

The pattern will tell you how to charge or load pick-up stick A. When you place the heddles in the down position, note that the ends pair up (photo 3). You will get different looks depending on which one of these pairs you pick up.

Sometimes you pick up the left yarn in each pair, which will place the yarns threaded through the back heddle holes to the top layer. Sometimes you will pick up the right yarn in each pair, which will bring the yarns threaded through the front holes to the top layer. Regardless, you always want to have the heddles in the down position so you pick up just the slot threads.

To charge pick-up stick B, place both heddles in the up position. Slide pick-up stick A toward the heddles so that it touches heddle 2. You will see 2 sheds—a small upper shed into which pick-up stick A is placed and a larger lower shed. Place pick-up stick B in the lower shed (photo 4). If the shed isn't clean, meaning warp yarns are sticking to one another within the shed, move pick-up stick A back and forth until you get a clean shed.

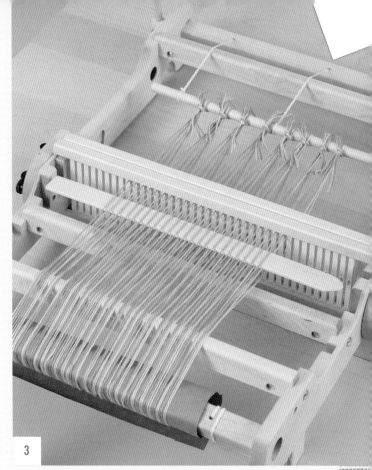

Charge pick-up stick A by placing the heddles in the down position and picking up the appropriate ends.

To charge pick-up stick B, place the heddles in the up position and slide pick-up stick A to the back of the heddles. Slide pick-up stick B between the upper and lower layers.

Warping

1   Warp your loom using the recommended 2-heddle warping method (see Chapter Nine). Refer to the warping and threading schematic for the warp color order and threading information.

Weaving

2   Wind 2 shuttles with a generous amount of each color weft yarn, an additional shuttle with 15 yd (14 m) of pink weft yarn, and 1 shuttle with scrap yarn.

3   Weave a 1"–2" (2.5–5 cm) header of smooth scrap yarn to spread your warp (see Chapter Two).

PLACE PICK-UP STICKS

4   Place both heddles in the down position. Working behind the heddles, pick up every other warp end, starting with the first up end.

5   Place both heddles in the up position. Slide pick-up stick A toward the heddles so that it touches heddle 2. Place pick-up stick B in the lowest shed, behind the heddles.

JOIN THE LAYERS

6   The layers are joined by weaving plain weave which requires lifting and lowering both heddles together. Start with the tan weft yarn, leaving

a tail 6 times the width of your warp. Weave 1" (2.5 cm) of plain weave using the tan weft and ending on a down shed.

7   Work a row of hemstitching (see Chapter Ten) to secure the beginning of the cloth.

WEAVE PILLOW COVER BODY

8   There are 4 picks in the pattern repeat for the pillow-cover body. Weave the first tubular double-weave pattern. Starting on the right side, engage pick-up stick B by placing the heddles in neutral and tipping the pick-up stick on its edge. Weave the first pick (lower layer).

9   Lay pick-up stick B flat and push it to the back of the loom. Place heddle 2 in the up position and weave the second pick (upper layer).

10   Place heddle 1 in the down position. Weave a third pick (upper layer).

11   With the heddles in neutral, engage pick-up stick A and weave the fourth pick (lower layer).

12   Repeat Steps 9–12, weaving for 11¼" (28.5 cm) using the tan weft yarn.

    After weaving 3" (7.5 cm), stop to check that both your seams are connected and that you haven't inadvertently attached the layers. Place heddle 2 in the up position and pull pick-up stick A forward until it touches heddle 2. This will lift the upper layer above the lower layer.

13   Repeat Steps 9–12 again, but this time weave 11¼" (28.5 cm) using the pink weft yarn.

WEAVE THE FLAP

14   Weave 2" (5 cm) with the selvedges not connected. Weave the lower layer with the first shuttle and the upper layer with the second shuttle.

15   Continue weaving the same sequence in pink, but introduce a second shuttle wound with pink yarn as follows:

STEP 1 Using the working weft, weave the first pick in your pattern repeat as you have been doing in the pick-up stick B shed.

STEP 2 Place heddle 2 in the up position and introduce your second shuttle by laying it in from the right, leaving a '6" (15.2 cm) tail.

TUBULAR DOUBLE-WEAVE PATTERN

Work tubular doubleweave over 4 picks:

1   Pick-up stick B (lower layer).
2   Heddle 2 up (upper layer).
3   Heddle 1 down (lower layer).
4   Pick-up stick A (upper layer).

STEP 3 Place heddle 1 in the down position and weave a third pick with the first shuttle.

STEP 4 With the heddles in neutral, engage pick-up stick A and weave the fourth pick with the second shuttle, tucking your tail into this shed.

16 Hemstitch the ends of the flap so that they are secure while finishing the pillow.

17 Place the heddles in neutral and remove the pick-up sticks. Cut a length of weft yarn 4 times the width of your fabric from the second shuttle and hemstitch over 2 warps and 2 wefts.

18 Place heddle 2 in the up position and pull pick-up stick A toward the front of the loom until it is touching heddle 2 to lift the upper layer above the lower layer.

19 Cut the upper layer from the loom, leaving the lower layer attached. Fold the upper layer out of the way and work a row of hemstitching along the lower layer.

Finishing

20 Remove the cloth from the front beam. Trim any tails to 2" (5 cm). Check the cloth for any skips and fix before washing (see Chapter Ten).

21 Machine wash the pillow cover on the gentle cycle with ¼ cup mild detergent. Lay flat to dry.

22 Trim fringe to ¼" (6 mm) from the hemstitching and any tails flush with the cloth.

23 Turn the pillow cover inside out so that the closed end's plain-weave flap is on the inside. Place the pillow form inside the cover.

24 Fold the flaps of the open end to the inside of the pillow cover.

To secure the seam, you can either sew it shut using the invisible join (see Chapter Ten) with pink weft yarn, or add a zipper if you wish to remove the pillow form for future washings.

WARP COLOR ORDER

1) Sley 4 ends per slot in heddle 2 using the colors indicated. There are 34 tan and pink ends each in 17 slots; 108 cream ends, in 26 slots; 2 cream and pink each in one slot, and 86 tan and pink ends each in 43 slots.

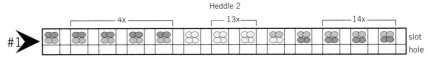

2) Move one end in the color indicated to the hole directly to the right of each filled slot, in the same heddle. Add heddle 1 in front of heddle 2.

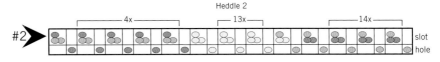

3) a) Working right to left, thread the end that is in the first hole in heddle 2 into the slot immediately to the right of the corresponding hole in heddle 1, as shown in schematic 3.
b) Move the next 3 slot ends in heddle 2 to heddle 1 using this schematic as a guide. The pink end joins it mate in the slot. The tan ends are threaded hole/slot.

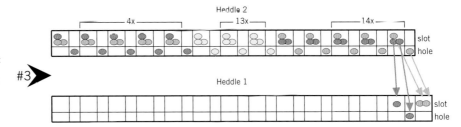

4) Continue working the two steps outlined in step 3 and following the color order shown in schematic 4: Move the hole end in heddle 2, to the slot at right of the corresponding hole in heddle 1. Then move the three slotted ends in heddle 2, slot, hole, slot in heddle 1.

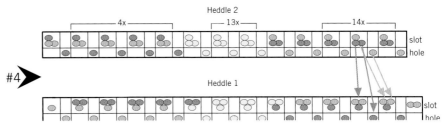

CHAPTER SEVEN

THE BATHROOM

Bathrooms are a good place to use linens with more decorative patterns that make everyday routines magical. I am particularly fond of decorative fingertip towels that your guests are more likely to see than kitchen towels, so I focus make them extra fancy. Also, facecloths make great gifts and a relaxing bath feel more like a spa treatment. Bathmats are functional, and I love the look of them draped over the side of the tub or as a way to brighten up the floor.

Linen FACECLOTHS

These luxurious facecloths will be your go-to gift-giving project as well as a daily joy in your life. Made with linen yarns, they gently exfoliate the skin, leaving it smooth and soft. Linen yarns are the perfect material for weaving facecloths because linen holds up well wash after wash and dries quickly. Here, a lacy windowpane structure worked in two weights of linen to create deeper cells provides the perfect textured surface for that little touch of handmade beauty in your daily routine.

PROJECT SPECS

FINISHED SIZE
Two cloths, each 10¾" x 10½" (27.5 x 26.6 cm).

WEAVE STRUCTURE
Windowpane.

EQUIPMENT
12-dent rigid-heddle loom with a 13" (33 cm) weaving width; 4 stick shuttles; 15" (38 cm) pick-up stick.

NOTIONS
Sewing thread and needle; scrap yarn; liquid sealant such as Fray Check (optional).

WARP AND WEFT SPECIFICATIONS

SETT (EPI)
12.

WEAVING WIDTH
12" (30.5 cm).

PICKS PER INCH (PPI)
14.

WARP LENGTH
48" (122 cm; includes 20" [50.8 cm] for loom waste and take-up).

NUMBER OF ENDS
145 (37 thick, 108 thin).

RECOMMENDED WARPING METHOD
Indirect.

YARNS

Warp: 4-ply sportweight wet-spun linen (1,300 yd [1,189 m]/lb): 50 yd (46 m) pale lavender; 2-ply lace-weight wet-spun linen (2,600 yd [2,377 m]/lb): 144 yd (132 m) light gray.

Shown here: Louet Euroflax Sport (100% wet-spun linen, 270 yd [247 m]]/3½ oz skein): Soft Violet; Louet Euroflax Lace (100% wet-spun linen, 630 yd [576 m]/3¾ oz mini cone): #18.2212-2 Cloud Grey.

Weft: 4-ply sportweight wet-spun linen: 22 yd (20 m) pale lavender; 2-ply laceweight wet-spun linen: 56 yd (51 m) light gray, 56 yd (51 m) dark gray.

Shown here: Louet Euroflax Sport: Soft Violet; Louet Euroflax Lace: Cloud Grey, Heron Grey.

Warping

1   Warp your loom following the project specs using the Warp Color Order chart.

TIP: *The warp must start and end in a slot for the windowpane pattern to be centered within the thin warp ends.*

Weaving

2   Wind 1 shuttle with the lavender accent weft yarn, 1 shuttle with the light gray weft yarn, 1 shuttle with the dark gray weft yarn, and 1 shuttle with a generous amount of scrap yarn.

3   Weave 1" (2.5 cm) of scrap yarn to spread your warp (see Chapter Two).

4   Using the light gray weft yarn, leave a tail 6 times the width of your warp and weave your first pick in an up shed.

5   Weave 7 more picks, ending in a down shed. Work a row of hemstitching (see Chapter Ten) using the weft tail over 2 warp ends and 2 weft picks to secure the work after it is taken off the loom.

    Alternately, you can use a liquid seam sealer such as Fray Check to secure the ends, leaving a smaller tail and tucking it in as you weave.

NOTE: *It's important to secure the ends of the yarn before you take the cloth off the loom, whether you stitch them or seal them. In this lacy structure, linen yarns have a tendency to work their way out of the fabric once it is taken off the loom and the warp is trimmed for hemming.*

6   Charge the pick-up stick by placing the heddle in the down position, picking up all the lavender warps behind the rigid heddle.

WORK PATTERN REPEATS

7   Work 1 repeat of the Windowpane Pattern using the thick lavender yarn as your accent thread as follows:

STEP 1 *Up:* Weave 1 pick of light gray weft with the heddle up.

STEP 2 *Pick-up stick:* Place the heddle in neutral and tip the pick-up stick on its edge. Add the lavender accent thread by placing it in this shed. To create a nice flat edge, manually pick up the third warp end from each selvedge. Use the ply-splitting technique (see Chapter Two) to integrate the tail.

STEP 3 *Up:* Change to an up shed and weave with the light gray weft.

STEP 4 *Down:* Change to a down shed and weave with the light gray weft.

STEP 5 *Up and pick-up stick:* Place the rigid heddle in an up shed and, keeping it flat, slide the pick-up stick forward until it touches the heddle. Weave a light gray pick.

STEP 6 *Down:* Weave a down pick with the light gray weft yarn.

TIP: *Carry the accent weft up the side of the work until you are ready to weave with it again.*

8   Repeat Pattern Steps 1–6 twenty-six more times.

9   End the weaving by working the first 2 steps of the Windowpane Pattern—up and pick-up stick sheds—so that you end on an accent thread.

    Cut the accent thread and use the ply-splitting technique to integrate the tail.

10   Weave 8 picks of plain weave using the thin weft yarn. You will have woven about 13" (33 cm) of cloth.

11   Secure the ends with another row of hemstitching to stabilize the fringe or apply liquid seam sealer.

12   Weave 2" (5 cm) of scrap yarn.

13   Repeat Steps 4–12 to make the second linen-facecloth, substituting the dark gray weft yarn for the light gray weft yarn.

Finishing

14   Remove the fabric from the loom. Cut the 2 face-cloths apart and trim tails to 2" (5 cm). Trim the warp to ¼" (6 mm) from the stitching.

15   Place the fabric right side down—the side that was facing you as you wove. Fold the end over 2 picks below the fringe and then fold again ¼" (6 mm) to encase the fringe. Pin the seam to secure for stitching. Use coordinating sewing thread to whipstitch the fold in place (see Chapter Ten).

16   Machine wash on the gentle cycle in hot water with a regular detergent. If you have a terry-cloth towel, wash it with the facecloths to provide some additional agitation and protect the cloth from the agitator. Lay flat to dry. Trim remaining tails flush with the cloth.

WARP COLOR ORDER

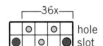

● Thick pale lavender
○ Thin light gray

WINDOWPANE PATTERN

Work the Windowpane Pattern over these 6 steps:

1   Up.
2   Pick-up stick (accent weft).
3   Up.
4   Down.
5   Up and pick-up stick.
6   Down.

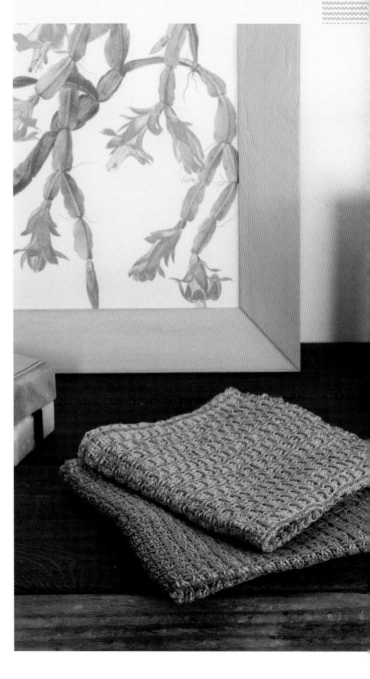

Bordering on Perfect HAND TOWELS

Working fancy borders on a plain-weave ground is a great way to play with color and pattern. Intricate patterns worked for just a few inches (or several centimeters) pop off the ground cloth. You can use this technique with any number of pick-up patterns. In the case of these hand towels, the back of the pattern is just as interesting as the front—you can show off both sides of this project.

PROJECT SPECS

FINISHED SIZE
Two towels about 13" x 21" (33 x 53.5 cm).

WEAVE STRUCTURES
Pick-up and plain weave.

EQUIPMENT
10-dent rigid-heddle loom with a 16" (40.5 cm) weaving width; 5 stick shuttles; 16" (40.5 cm) pick-up stick.

NOTIONS
Sewing thread; sewing needle; scrap yarn.

WARP AND WEFT SPECIFICATIONS

SETT (EPI)
10.

WEAVING WIDTH
15" (38 cm).

PICKS PER INCH (PPI)
10 plain weave, 22 pattern.

WARP LENGTH
76" (193 cm; includes 23" [58.5 cm] for loom waste and take-up).

NUMBER OF WARP ENDS
151.

RECOMMENDED WARPING METHOD
Direct.

YARNS

Warp: 3/2 unmercerized cotton (1,260 yd [1,152 m]/lb): 320 yd (293 m) brown.

Shown here: Lunatic Fringe 3/2 American Maid Naturally Colored Cotton (100% unmercerized cotton; 630 yd [576 m]/8 oz cone): Dark Brown.

Ground Weft: 3/2 unmercerized cotton: 184 yd (168 m) brown.

Shown here: Lunatic Fringe 3/2 American Maid Naturally Colored Cotton: Dark Brown.

Pattern Weft: 3/2 unmercerized cotton: 15 yd (14 m) each light green, dark green; 8/2 unmercerized cotton (3,360 yd [3,072 m]/lb): 62 yd (57 m) brown.

Shown here: Lunatic Fringe 3/2 American Maid Naturally Colored Cotton: Light Green and Dark Green; Lunatic Fringe 8/2 American Maid Naturally Colored Cotton (100% unmercerized cotton, 1,680 yd [1,536 m]/8 oz cone): Dark Brown.

Warping

1 Warp your loom following the project specs and using the direct method.

NOTE: *The warp must start and end in a heddle hole to balance the pick-up pattern in the slots.*

Weaving

2 Wind 3 shuttles with each of the three colors of 3/2 cotton ground and pattern weft yarn, 1 shuttle with 8/2 brown pattern weft yarn, and 1 shuttle with scrap yarn.

3 Prepare a paper guide (see Chapter Two) with the following measurements: 1¾" (4.5 cm) hem, 2" (5 cm) plain weave ground, 2¾" (7 cm) pattern, 18" (45.5 cm) plain weave ground, 1¾" (4.5 cm) hem.

4 Weave a 1" (2.5 cm) header of scrap yarn to spread your warp (see Chapter Two).

5 Leaving a tail 6 times the width of your warp, and starting in an up shed, weave 1¾" (4.5 cm) with the brown 8/2 cotton for the hem.

6 Thread the tail through a tapestry needle and work a row of embroidery stitch (see Chapter Ten) to secure the beginning.

7 Fasten off the 8/2 brown cotton, change to the thicker 3/2 cotton brown weft yarn, and weave 2" (5 cm) of plain weave, ending with a down shed.

8 Fasten off the 3/2 cotton and add the 8/2 brown cotton weft back in for the border pattern.

PLACE THE PICK-UP STICK

9 Place the heddle in the down position and pick up the slot threads in the following order:

3 up, 1 down, 1 up, 1 down, 4 up

[1 down, 1 up] x 2

1 down, 5 up

[1 down, 1 up] x 3

1 down, 6 up

[1 down, 1 up] x 4

1 down, 6 up

[1down, 1 up] x 3

1 down, 5 up

[1 down, 1 up] x 2

1 down, 4 up, 1 down, 1 up, 1 down, 3 up

10 Beginning in an up shed, using the 8/2 cotton and the dark green 3/2 cotton, weave the Hand Towel Border Pattern.

When indicated, weave multiple picks in the pick -up shed, taking your shuttle around the selvedge thread to lock the weft in at the edges. Interlock the working and nonworking wefts as you weave.

11 Repeat the pattern using the light green weft yarn.

12 Weave 18" (45.5 cm) plain-weave ground with the 3/2 cotton ground weft yarn.

13 Finish with 1¾" (4.5 cm) with the brown 8/2 cotton weft yarn.

14 Work a row of embroidery stitch (see Chapter Ten) to secure the weft.

15 Leave 2" (5 cm) of open warp. Following Steps 5–14, weave a second towel as you did the first, reversing the color order of the pattern, starting with the light green yarn and ending with the dark green yarn.

Finishing

16 Remove the cloth from the loom. Trim any tails to 2" (5 cm). Trim the fringe to ¼" (6 mm).

17 Fold the end over ¼" (6 mm) and then fold again ½" (1.3 cm) to encase the fringe. Pin the seam to secure for stitching. Using coordinating sewing thread, machine or whipstitch the fold in place (see Chapter Ten).

18 Machine wash the towels on the gentle cycle in cool water with a regular detergent. Tumble dry on low and remove while still damp. Air- dry. Trim any weft wails flush with the fabric.

TIP: *Add a teaspoon of baking soda to the cool water if you want to speed up the darkening of the naturally colored cotton.*

HAND TOWEL BORDER PATTERN

Use the 8/2 brown pattern weft yarn and the 3/2 green pattern weft yarn for the border pattern:

1   Up.
2   Pick-up stick.
3   Up.
4   Down.
5   2 x pick-up stick.
6   Up.
7   Down.
8   3 x pick-up stick.
9   Up.
10 Down.
11 4 x pick-up stick.
12 Up.
13 Down.
14 3 x pick-up stick.
15 Up.
16 Down 8/2.
17 2 x pick-up stick.
18 Up.
19 Down.
20 Pick-up stick.

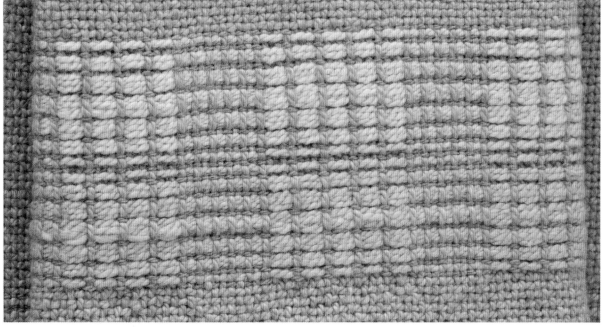

Two-Color **KROKBRAGD RUG**

Knit remnants make great rag rugs. Reclaimed from manufacturing waste, they can be found in lots of bright colors that are put up in continuous strips. In this rug, I worked knit remnants in a bright, nontraditional two-color Krokbragd, a weft-faced twill-like weave that has a strikingly different appearance on the front and back. You will fall in love with this structure for its terrific patterning possibilities.

PROJECT SPECS

FINISHED SIZE
One 16¼" x 29" (41.5 x 73.5 cm) Krokbragd rug.

WEAVE STRUCTURE
Krokbragd.

EQUIPMENT
5-dent rigid-heddle loom with a 21" (53 cm) weaving width; four 18" (46 cm) stick shuttles; two 3" (7.5 cm) S-hooks; tapestry beater; 20" (51 cm) temple; heddle rod; 25 string heddles; 2 pick-up sticks.

NOTIONS
Tapestry needle; sewing thread and sewing needle; liquid seam sealant, such as Fray Check; 16" x 28¼" (40.5 x 72 cm) of nonslip floor padding; scrap yarn.

WARP AND WEFT SPECIFICATIONS

SETT (EPI)
5.

WEAVING WIDTH
20½" (52 cm).

PICKS PER INCH (PPI)
10.

WARP LENGTH
56" (142 cm; includes 25" [63.5 cm] loomwaste and take up).

NUMBER OF WARP ENDS
103.

RECOMMENDED WARPING METHOD
Direct.

YARNS

Warp: 8/4 cotton carpet warp (1,600 yd [1,463 m]/lb): 160 yd (146 m) light yellow.

Shown here: Cotton Clouds Rug Warp (100% unmercerized cotton; 8,002 yd [731 m]/8 oz #31 cone): Pear.

Weft: 8/4 cotton carpet warp: 80 yd (73 m) light yellow; knit rag remnants (80 yd [73m]/lb): 74 yd (68 m) salmon, 126 yd (115 m) blue.

Shown here: Cotton Clouds Rug Warp: Pear; Lion Brand Fettuccini (100% recycled knits: 55 yd [50 m]/11 oz cone [color availability varies with recycled products]).

Warping

1. Warp the loom following the project specs and using the direct method, starting and stopping the warp in a hole.

2. Weight the selvedges with 3" (7.5 cm) S-hooks by slipping the hooks over both selvedge threads and letting them hang off the back of the loom (see Chapter Two).

Weaving

3. Wind 2 stick shuttles, each with 1 color of knit rag remnants. Wind 1 stick shuttle with the carpet warp and the other with the scrap yarn.

4. Weave a 3" (7.5 cm) header of smooth, chunky scrap yarn to spread your warp (see Chapter Two).

5. Weave the yellow header at the beginning of the rug with the carpet warp and, leaving a tail 6 times the width of the fabric, weave 1¼" (3.2 cm) using the tapestry beater to pack the weft and cover the warp (see Chapter Two).

6. Work 1 row of hemstitching (see Chapter Ten) with the tail over 4 warp ends and 2 weft picks. Add a bead of liquid seam sealant on each stitch to keep the ends from moving during finishing. This edge will not be seen in the final cloth. Fasten off the carpet warp.

7. Insert pick-up sticks and a heddle rod following the instructions in the Krokbragd Pattern.

8. Start the first pick using the salmon-colored weft yarn, leaving a 6" (15 cm) tail. Beat in the pick, then open the same shed, wrap the salmon-colored weft yarn around the edge thread, and pull it back into the shed, leaving a 1" (2.5 cm) tail on the bottom of the rug to be clipped later.

9. Start the second pick on the opposite side of the rug from the starting point of the first pick, using the blue weft yarn. Leave a tail and tuck it into the same shed as for the first pick of salmon-colored yarn.

10. Continue to follow the Weave Color Order chart, maintaining the 3-pick rotation of the Krokbragd pattern as indicated.

11. Complete the Weave Color Order chart 10 times.

12. Fasten off your blue weft by weaving its tail into the last shed of blue for 5" (12.5 cm), pulling it out to the back of your rug, and then clipping it. Weave 1 more pick of salmon in a pick-up stick A shed, then fasten it off as the blue weft.

13. End with 1¼" (3.2 cm) of yellow carpet warp, securing it with hemstitching and liquid sealant.

Finishing

14. Remove the cloth from the loom, remove the scrap-yarn header, and trim tails flush with the fabric.

15. Fold each end over ¼" (6 mm), then fold again where the carpet warp header meets the pattern. Whipstitch in place (see Chapter Ten).

WEAVE COLOR ORDER

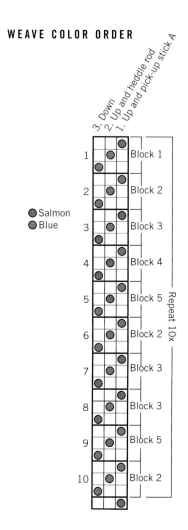

16   It is not necessary to wet-finish the rug. If it needs washing after use, fill a tub with lukewarm water and a small amount of a mild detergent and add the rug. Gently swish the rug in the water. Remove and refill the basin with clean water, add the rug and swish it to rinse. Remove the rug and roll it in a heavy towel to press out excess water. Lay flat to dry.

For safety, especially in the bathroom, place a piece of nonslip floor padding slightly smaller than your rug under it.

KROKBRAGD PATTERN

The Krokbragd Pattern is woven in 3-pick pattern repeats.

1   Up and pick-up stick A: Place heddle in the up position and slide the stick forward behind the heddle.

2   Up and heddle rod: Place heddle in the up position and pull up on the heddle rod to open the shed.

3   Down: Place heddle in the down position.

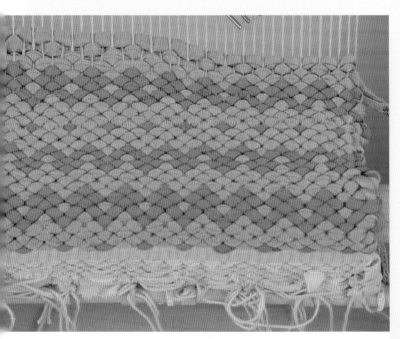

In a Krokbragd weaving, the design emerges only through tightly compacting the weaving.

WEAVING KROKBRAGD

Krokbragd is a fascinating weave that can be a little tricky to read until you get used to it. It is a weft-faced, twill-like weave that has a plain-weave pick thrown in every third pick. You can weave a 3-shaft Krokbragd on a rigid-heddle loom with 1 heddle and 2 pick-up sticks. Using a heddle rod simplifies the process by eliminating the need to recharge a pick-up stick every third pick.

Setup

To set up this project for the Krokbragd pattern, you need 2 pick-up sticks, 25 string heddles, and 1 heddle rod.

Pick-Up Stick A

Place the heddle in the down position and pick up the slot ends—1 up/1 down—across the width of the warp, ending with a down end. Place the stick behind the heddle.

Pick-Up Stick B

With the heddle still in the down position, pick up the slot ends in the opposite order—1 down/1 up. Place the heddle in neutral, tip pick-up stick B on its end, and place the up ends on the heddle rod (see Chapter Two).

Weaving

Krokbragd is woven in three steps:

1   Up and pick-up stick A.

2   Up and pick-up stick B (or heddle rod charged with pick-up stick B ends).

3   Down.

The picks don't build in the same way that you are used to seeing. Each set of 3 picks creates 2 rows of pattern rather than 3 rows of pattern.

The construction of this weave is very clever. It uses the first 2 picks of a 3-shaft twill, but instead of continuing the step progression, a plain-weave pick is thrown in every 2 picks. The 2 twill-based picks bend over this plain-weave pick to form this structure's unique look.

A Krokbragd is a weft-faced weave. You need to compact the rows regularly with a tapestry beater to see the pattern emerge. You can leave the fabric less compacted if you like that look and still have a perfectly acceptable rug with a hand similar to the Fabric Stash Rag Rug in Chapter Four.

CHAPTER EIGHT

WARP YOUR RIGID-HEDDLE LOOM

You can warp a rigid-heddle loom in one of two ways: direct or indirect. The direct method is the fastest and utilizes a warping peg. The indirect method is more versatile and utilizes a warping board. These techniques can be applied to warping one or more heddles.

Choosing Your Warping Technique

Many weavers learn the direct method of warping and use it as their sole means of warping. There is nothing wrong with this. It can be helpful to learn another way to warp your loom. You can certainly accomplish any given task with a single method, but a different technique may help you get the job done with better results.

DIRECT WARPING is easy to learn, fast, specific to rigid-heddle looms, and requires minimal equipment.

INDIRECT WARPING is more universal to many loom types, has more steps, takes a little longer, and requires more equipment. It allows you to work in a more compact area and, depending on your setup, more comfortably, particularly for long, fine, wide warps, which can make complicated color orders that require odd number of ends easier to manage.

Here is how I decided whether to use the direct or indirect warping method in these projects:

DIRECT

- Solid warps of a single yarn type
- Short warps of 3 yd (2.7 m) or less
- Stripes of even numbers of warp ends

INDIRECT

- Long warps of 3 yd (2.7 m) or more
- Complicated color orders
- Mixed warps
- Stripes with odd numbers of warp ends

Warping Two Rigid Heddles

Warping 2 heddles lets you weave finer fabrics and nifty patterns such as twill and doubleweave. Two heddles can be warped using either the direct or indirect method. The same rules apply to warping 2 heddles as warping a single heddle. I recommend direct warping for solid-colored warps and indirect warping for complicated color orders. The indirect method cuts down on the crossed threads in the back that can cause tension issues as you near the end of your warp. If you warp your 2 heddles using the direct method, consider adding some extra warp to mitigate these tension problems.

How to: Direct Warping

Setup

You need a rigid-heddle loom, one appropriately-sized rigid heddle, several clamps, a warping peg, a threading hook, warping yarn, scissors, craft paper, and a tape measure (photo 1).

1   Clamp the loom to a stable surface at a comfortable height. Then secure the warping peg so that it is facing the front of the loom at the desired distance away from the loom (photo 2). The distance between the peg and where you place the back apron rod will be your warp length.

   If your loom has a back beam, be sure that your apron rod is lifted over the beam. Adjust the apron cords so that they are traveling in a straight distance from the warp beam to the apron rod.

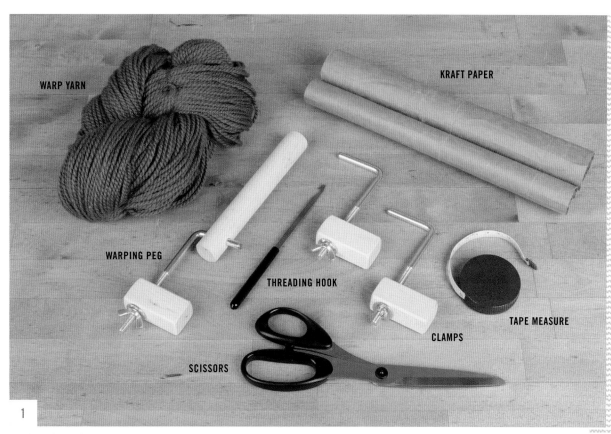

Gather these basic tools for direct warping your rigid-heddle loom.

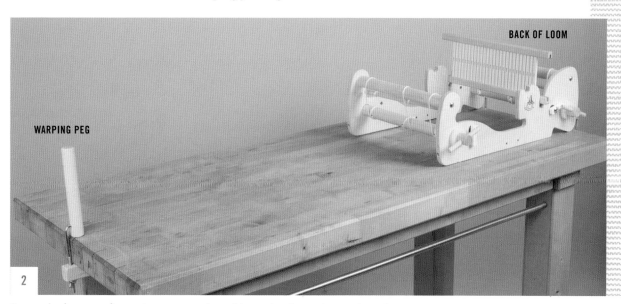

Space the loom and warping peg on the table at the desired warp length.

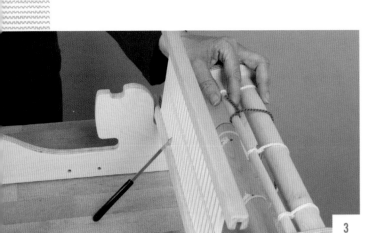

Tie the warp to the apron rod so it lines up with the correct slot.

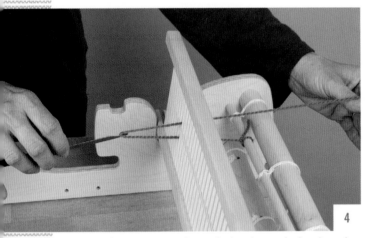

Pull the warp yarn through the slot with the threading hook.

Wrap the warp yarn around the apron rod.

2 Place the warp yarn on the floor near the apron rod. Find the middle of the rigid heddle and then-measure half your weaving width's distance from the center to find your starting point; this way, your project will be centered in the loom. Tie the working end to the apron rod so that it lines up with the appropriate slot on the rigid heddle (photo 3).

Thread the Slots with the Warp Yarn

3 Pull a loop of yarn through the first slot and place it on the warping peg on the opposite side of the table from your loom (photo 4).

4 Return to the back apron rod and wrap the yarn around the apron rod (avoid wrapping the back beam if you have one). Pull another loop of yarn through the slot next to the one you just threaded and place it on the warping peg, working toward the center of the rigid-heddle loom (photo 5).

TIP: *It doesn't matter if you go over or under the apron rod—the placement will alternate—what is most important is that you go around it. When you get to an apron cord, bring the yarn to the other side of the cord and keep working.*

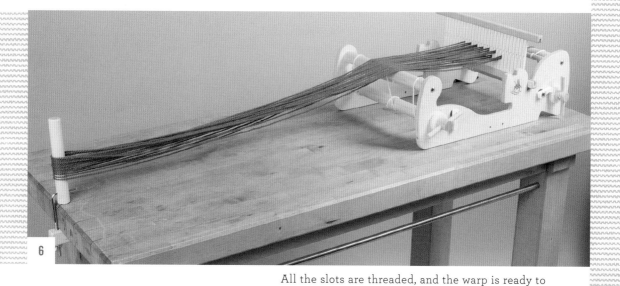

All the slots are threaded, and the warp is ready to be wound onto the warp beam.

5 Continue working in this manner until you have threaded the entire weaving width of your project (photo 6). Cut the yarn from the ball and tie the end to the apron rod using an overhand knot.

Wind Yarn onto the Warp Beam

6 Lift the yarn off the warping peg and cut the loops. Tie that end of the warp in an overhand knot to keep from inadvertently pulling on the individual ends. Let this end drop to the floor or table.

7 Laying craft paper between the layers, wind the warp onto the warp beam, stopping every few turns to tug on the warp in front of the overhand knot from the front to take up the slack (photo 7). Do not comb the warp with your fingers. If you have a snag, grab the entire warp with one hand and gently shake the warp to untangle (photo 8).

   Stop winding when you have 12" (30.5 cm) of warp in front of the heddle. Untie the overhand knot.

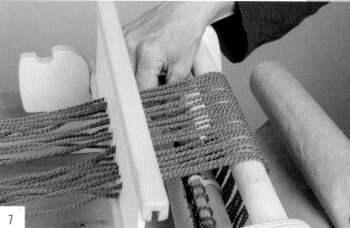

Use craft paper to separate the layers of warp as they are wound onto the warp beam.

Take up any slack in the warp by tugging on the yarn.

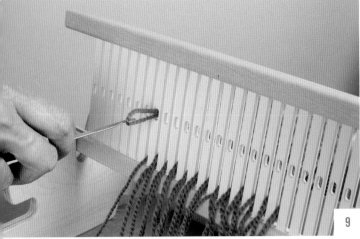

Remove one of the warp yarns from a slot and thread it through an adjacent hole.

Thread the Holes

8 Starting on 1 edge and working toward the other, remove 1 thread from each slot and thread it through an adjacent hole (photo 9).

Tie Warp Yarn onto the Front Apron Rod

9 Starting in the middle of the loom and working outward, tie 1" (2.5 cm) bundles of warp in the first half of a square knot around the apron rod (photos 10 and 11).

10 Work the other side of the loom in the same way until the entire warp is secured to the apron rod.

11 Working from one edge of the warp to the other, tighten the knots by pulling up on the ends to take up any slack. Check for even tension in the yarn by patting the warp with the palm of your hand, then tie the second half of the square knot to secure(photo 12).

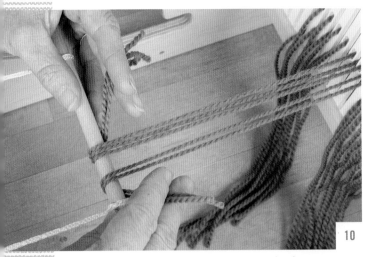

Tie the ends of the warp yarn to the front apron rod working the first half of a square knot.

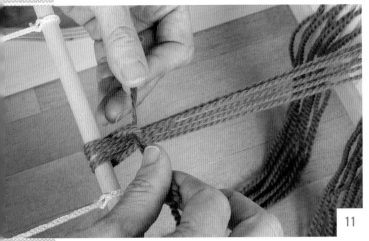

Adjust the knots for even tension, before tying the second half of the square knot.

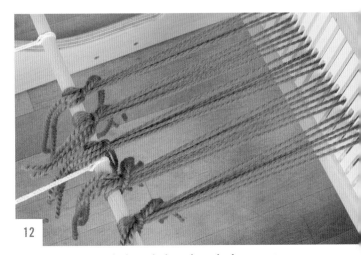

The warp is wound, threaded, and ready for weaving.

How to: Indirect Warping

Setup

You need a warping board, leader yarn, a threading hook, a measuring tape, kraft paper, scissors, and warp yarn.

Wind the Leader Yarn

1 To use a warping board, start by winding a yarn that contrasts with your warp yarn on the warping board in a path that is the same length as your warp.

2 Place your warp-yarn supply on the floor and use a slipknot to secure 1 end of the yarn to the peg where the leader yarn ends.

Wind the Warp

3 Follow the leader yarn with the warp yarn until you reach the first two pegs, then make a cross to keep the warp ends organized (photo 14).

   At the first two pegs, wind the warp yarn over the second peg and under the first, then over the first and under the second peg.

4 Follow the established path to the last peg, wind the yarn around that peg, then continue back up to the first row and wind another cross.

5 Continue in this manner until you have wound the total number of warp ends you need for your project. When the entire warp has been wound, wrap the end a few times around the final peg, then cut the strand.

6 Measure the length from the warp beam to the front apron rod. Use this measurement to cut a length of your contrasting leader yarn, then tie a choke on your warp (photo 15). The choke should

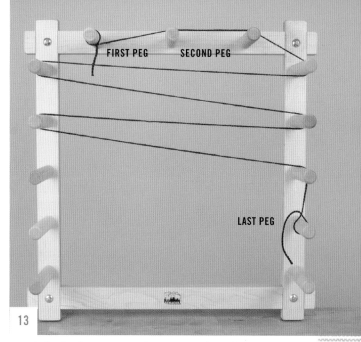

Wind the leader yarn on the warping board.

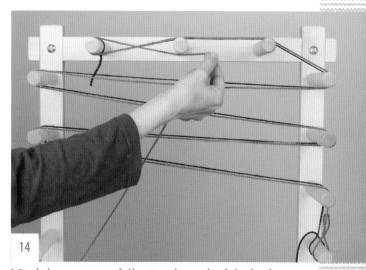

Wind the warp yarn following the path of the leader yarn.

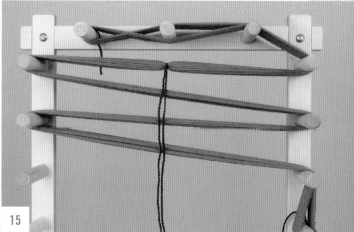

After the entire warp has been wound, tie a choke on the warp using a contrasting-colored yarn.

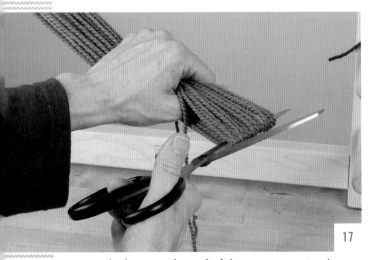

16

Maintain the cross in your hand as you carefully remove the warp from the warping board.

17

Cut the loops at the end of the warp opposite the cross end.

be the same distance from the front peg as your apron rod is from the warp beam.

Thread the Rigid Heddle with the Warp

7 Place the rigid heddle in the neutral position in the loom. Have a threading hook, scissors, and a tape measure handy.

8 Cut the single loops at the end opposite the cross, then tie them into an overhand knot (photo 16).

9 Secure the cross in your nondominant hand by placing your thumb in the right side of the cross, your index finger on the top, your ring finger on the bottom, and your middle finger in the left side as you gently slide the cross off the pegs (photo 17).

10 Carefully transfer the warp from the warping board to your loom.

11 Tie the choke on either the cloth or front beam, depending on your loom type (photo 18). If you have a lot of warp, drape it over the beam off to the side of the choke. The choke beam and overhand knot will keep it secure.

12 Cut the loop at the top of the cross so that you have a stack of loose ends in your palm (photo 19). The cross will keep them orderly as you work.

13 Starting with enough offset to the right or left side so that your warp is centered, pull 1 thread from

18

Use the choke tie to attach the warp to the front beam.

19

Hold the loops of the cross in the palm of your hand.

the cross and then thread it through the appropriate slot or hole following your project's color order (photo 20).

TIP: *If you are winding multiple colors, you may find it useful to wind each color separately, leaving spaces for the other colors.*

14 Continue working until your rigid heddle is threaded. Check for errors.

15 Tie the warp onto the warp beam using the same technique used to secure the warp to the front beam in the direct method. It is not necessary to check for even tension.

16 Cut the choke tie and wind onto the warp beam using craft paper between layers.

17 Tie onto the front as you did in the back, this time checking for even tension.

18 Follow Steps 9-12 of the direct warping method to finish.

20

Thread the warp through the slots and holes.

Threading Two Rigid Heddles

The steps for warping two heddles is very similar to warping one heddle, but with one very important difference—threading the heddles.

Setup

1   Place a rigid heddle in the heddle block farthest away from the front beam. This will eventually be your back heddle (heddle 2).

Direct Method

2   If using the direct method, instead of threading 1 loop of yarn through each slot, thread 2. Then wind on. Working from the front of the loom, move 1 of these 4 ends to the hole on its right.

NOTE: *Your pattern should tell you in what color order to thread your project. In the example shown here, 2 gray ends are threaded with 2 pinkends.*

Indirect Method

To warp 2 heddles using the indirect method, wind your warp on the warping board and then thread the heddle so that 1 thread is in every hole and 3 threads are in every slot. Tie the threads onto the back apron rod and wind onto the back beam. Be sure to follow any color order specifications as outlined in your pattern.

Threading the Heddles

From here on out, the method is the same for both styles of warping.

3   Place the front heddle (heddle 1) in front of the back heddle (heddle 2). Give yourself plenty of room to reach between the heddles to work.

NOTE: *You may work sitting at the front or the back of the loom. The photographs are showing the action as viewed from the back.*

Starting on the right side of the heddle, take the first yarn threaded in a hole in the back heddle and thread it through the slot to the left of

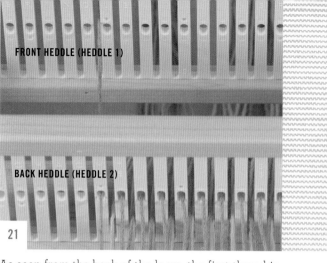

FRONT HEDDLE (HEDDLE 1)

BACK HEDDLE (HEDDLE 2)

21

As seen from the back of the loom, the first thread in the back heddle is threaded to the slot to the left of the corresponding hole in the front heddle.

the corresponding hole in the front heddle (photo 21).

TIP: *It can help to stand up and look straight down between the heddles when you do this. Be sure to line up this first thread correctly or you won't be able to get a good shed.*

4   Take the next 3 ends threaded in the slot in the back heddle and thread them as follows:
   • First end in the slot that is already threaded (photo 22)
   • Second end in the hole to its left (photo 23)
   • Third end in the next slot to the left (photo 24).

5   Continue working in this manner, threading the yarn in the hole in the back to the slot to the right of the corresponding hole and then the 3 ends in the slot or hole as outlined above.

   All the yarns threaded in the back heddle should go through a slot in the front heddle and vice versa.

6   After you have completed the threading, tie onto the front apron rod as you would with either the direct or indirect method.

NOTE: *Threading 2 heddles seems more complicated than it really is. If you are a visual learner, check out my two video workshops: Twice as Nice: Weaving With Two Heddles on a Rigid-Heddle Loom or Double Your Fun: Doubleweave on a Rigid-Heddle Loom.*

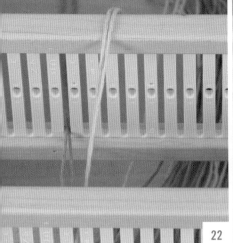

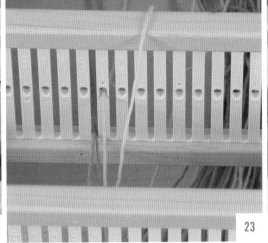

22 | 23 | 24

Take one of the 3 ends threaded in the next slot in the back heddle and place it in the same slot in the front heddle, which is already threaded.

Thread the second slotted end in the back heddle (heddle 2) in the hole to the right of the threaded slot.

Thread the third slotted end in the back heddle in the next open slot to the right in the front heddle.

THE RELATIONSHIP BETWEEN TWO HEDDLES AND FOUR SHAFTS

As demonstrated by the projects in this book, I love using 2 heddles to achieve finer setts, easily achievable twill patterns, and doubleweave.

By threading 2 heddles, you create a straight draw used to weave many 4-shaft patterns. Due to the nature of the slot and hole construction of the rigid heddle loom, this draft charts a straight draw with all the possible related rigid-heddle positions using 2 heddles and 2 pick-up sticks set up as they would be for a 1/3 twill. (See the Twill Be Done Runner in Chapter Five for information on how to read a draft.) This configuration allows each end in the 4-thread straight draw threading sequence to be lifted individually.

With a bit of patience and determination, you can weave most 4-shaft patterns threaded on a straight draw with 2 heddles and 2 pick-up sticks—but it is not necessarily easy. It can be a fun challenge to figure out if you can weave various drafts with 2 heddles based on the rigid-heddle positions you can achieve with your loom.

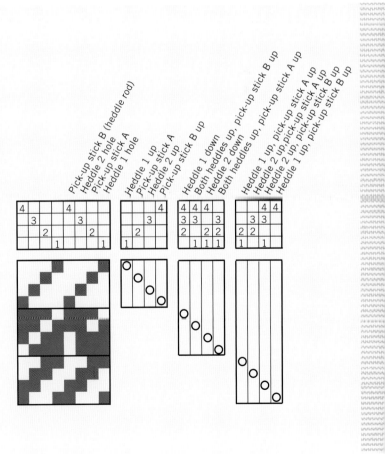

TIPS FOR WARPING WIDE, LONG, AND FINE WARPS

Weaving for the home often requires that you put on wide warps or long warps or warp with relatively fine threads. In some cases all three! Here are a few tips for dealing with those situations:

Wide Warps

If using the direct method, it can be helpful to use more than 1 warping peg (photo 1). This allows the warp yarn to travel a relatively straight path between the rigid-heddle loom and the peg, avoiding any foreshortening that can happen with steep angles.

If you are using the indirect method, wind the warp in more than one chunk, then divide the warp in half or in thirds. Warp the loom in sections, tying each section to the front beam with its own choke tie. This also allows the warp yarns to travel in a relatively straight line from the front beam to the rigid heddle.

Weaving Width

We weavers have a tendency to want to max out our warping width, but winding a tidy warp requires that you have some space to work with on either side of the warp to place your craft paper or sticks. This extra room will also come in handy when warping a long warp. If possible, use a loom wider than your project.

Long Warps

If you are using the direct method and you want to warp a particularly long warp, consider investing in a warping board or some sort of peg board (photo 2). Such a tool will keep the distance that the warp has to travel to a minimum and make the warping process more manageable.

Instead of bringing the loops of yarn to the peg, find a path on the warping board that matches your warp length and wind each end accordingly, looping the yarn on the appropriate peg. Remove the yarn as you would on a single peg. Then, when ready, hold the loops in your hand and cut the yarn from the warping board.

Long warps can become unwieldy if not contained in some way. Consider chaining your warp as you remove it from the warping board, whether you are using the direct or indirect method (photo 3). Cut the ends as usual and tie an overhand knot (for the indirect method, this is the end opposite the cross.) Place your hand inside the loop and pull a length of warp through the loop to form another loop (photo 4). Continue to pull loops through as if you were crocheting a large chain. Stop 24" (61 cm) from the cross if you are using the indirect warping method or from the front beam if you are using the direct method.

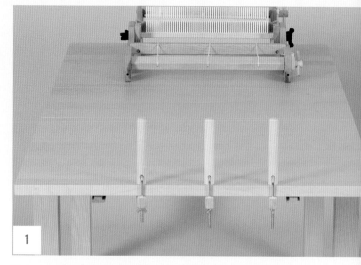

Using multiple warping pegs will keep your warp ends from being uneven when using the direct warping method for wide warps.

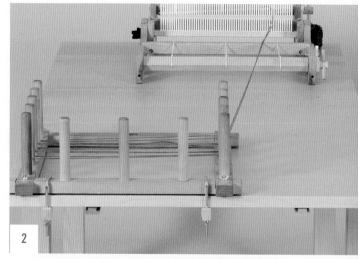

A warping board makes it easier to wind a very long warp in a small space when using the direct method.

Chaining long warps keep them tidy while winding on. Form a loop at the end of the warp.

Pull the warp through the loop to form a slipknot.

If you are using the indirect method, place the last loop on your hand that will hold the cross, transfer the cross as well to that hand and move the chain to the loom to start threading. If you are using the direct method, drape the loop over the front beam or let it fall to the floor.

Fine Warps

It is even more important that you treat a warp as a unit and resist raking or pulling on individual threads with fine warps.

If you are using a relatively fine laceweight yarn, you may want to use warping sticks instead of craft paper between the layers wound on the back beam (photo 5). The sticks provide a hard surface for the yarns to wind on. All paper has some give that allows the yarn to sink slightly as it is packed onto the beam. This is not a problem with yarns that have a thicker grist.

Maximum Warp Length

A lot of weavers ask, "How much warp can I pack on my beam?" The answer is, "It depends." Your loom type and the thickness of your yarn dictate how much yarn you can pack on your beams. However, the real question isn't how much unwoven warp can you pack on your warp beam, but how much woven cloth can you fit on your cloth beam. Woven cloth is thicker than the unwoven warp alone. Even if you can fit a long warp on your warp beam, you may reach a point where, depending on your loom, the woven fabric rolled up on the cloth beam will start interfering with the warp, preventing you from getting a good shed. As a general guideline, I suggest not exceeding 3 yards (2.75 meters) for worsted/DK weight yarns and more than 5 yards (4.5 meters) for fine laceweight yarns, but it depends on your loom.

5

Use warping sticks instead of paper to separate layers of warp on the back beam with extremely inelastic or super fine yarns.

CHAPTER NINE

FINISH YOUR WEAVING

You're done! Well almost—now you need to finish. The projects in this book range from simple to fancy. To finish strong, you want to pick the finish that fits your style, the yarn's attributes, and the project's final function. Removing the cloth from the loom, securing the fringe, and washing all take a bit of know-how. It is the icing on our cake.

Finishing Strong

For some folks, their love of weaving is just that—they love the act of passing the shuttle back and forth and placing the weft. Warping and finishing aren't in the same bucket, but they are as much a part of weaving as the middle part.

I love the handwork involved in creating a line of hemstitching or making a decorative knotted fringe almost as much as I enjoy making the cloth itself. There is a special satisfaction that comes with finding the perfect finish—whether elaborate or simple—to complement your weaving. Regardless of how you finish, do all your finishing work before you wash your cloth.

Removing the Fabric

Before you can finish the cloth, you need to carefully remove it from the loom. I typically cut the fabric from the loom behind the rigid heddle. I always untie from the front so I don't risk cutting an apron cord.

Remove the header and do all of finishing work before you wash it. Trim any weft tails to 2" (5 cm) so they don't snag in the wash. Leave fringe long and trim it to length after washing.

Fixing Floats

Examine the cloth carefully and repair any skips by needleweaving in a short repair thread that follows the correct path that the weft should have taken (photo 1). Weave a generous amount of supplemental weft on either side of the float to increase its stability, leaving a 2" (5 cm) tail of yarn on either side of the repair.

After the fabric is washed, you can trim the float away. If you have missed a step in a weaving sequence, say twill for example, where you forgot to weave one of the rows, this can also be fixed in a similar fashion.

1

You can fix a missing float by weaving a thread in the path of the missing thread.

To fix it, determine the path of the missing thread and needleweave a new thread in the correct path across the entire width of the warp. Needleweave the tails into the cloth following the pick above or below the repair.

Hemming Handwovens

Towels, runners, and other hard-wearing household goods are generally hemmed. Looking from a design perspective, bulk at the hems should be decreased as much as possible to enable the textile to lay or hang flat and to not call too much attention to the hem. To this end, you can weave your hems with a finer yarn than your warp.

You can secure the ends either on the loom with a quick row of embroidery or hemstitching or off the loom using a serger or a straight stitch. Either way, I recommend securing the weft before you trim the fringe for hemming to ensure that your warp and weft don't start to wander, giving you a messy edge.

NOTE: *It is easier to use a sewing machine on fine, dense, evenly spaced fabrics than it is on chunky, open lace work. In most instances, I prefer to work hems by hand, but your skill at the sewing machine may be better than mine. Use whatever skills are in your toolbox to get the job done!*

The only instance you may want to wash before sewing is when hemming by machine. The fabric shrinks and becomes more uniform in the wash. Depending on your technique, machine sewn fabric may pucker at the seams after washing.

HOW TO: HEM

1 Using a rotary cutter and a self-healing mat, trim the fringe ¼" (6 mm) (photo 2). Fold over the end of the fabric ¼" (6 mm), then finger press the fold in place or take the extra step of steam-pressing it. Following the instructions for the project, fold again and pin (photo 3). Press.

   If you choose to machine sew the hem, pin your fabric perpendicular to the edge with the heads on the outside so that you can easily remove them as you work (this is essentially the opposite of what is shown in photo 3). Take care to adjust your sewing machine's tension appropriately for the fabric thickness and style.

2 If you're hemming your project by hand, cut a length of thread 3 times the width of your cloth. Thread a sewing needle, then knot the end. Double the thread, stopping just short of the knot to decrease the thread length while working.

3 To handsew your hem, bring your needle and thread up through the inside of 1 folded corner. Hide the knotted end in the seam. Sew the sides of the hem together by catching the outside selvedges, starting on the same side each time. If you start on the right, the needle will always enter the cloth from the right. Finish sewing the side seam of the hem.

4 Next, work a whipstitch along the length of the cloth with a coordinating sewing thread (contrasting shown for demonstration purposes), catching 1 weft thread just under the fold on the cloth and then 1 weft thread at the edge of the fold. Catch the same weft threads each time as you sew a stitch.

5 Sew the other side seam in place. Bury the thread in the seam by entering the needle at 1 corner and bringing it out the stitched side of the seam.

6 Knot the thread at the base of the seam. Place the needle under the hem and bring it out 2" (5 cm) away from the knot. Cut the thread where it exits the cloth.

   Using this method, your stitching will be barely visible and your hems secure.

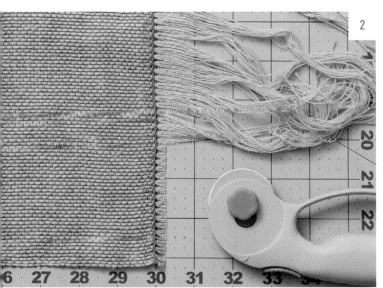

Cut the fringe ¼" (6mm) before encasing it in the hem.

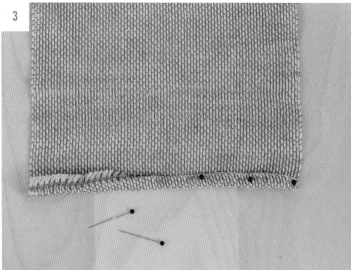

Fold the hem twice, then pin it before stitching it down.

Joins and Seams

It can be challenging to seam relatively thick fabrics together invisibly. I prefer to seam my fabrics so that the seams become part of the finishing. You can see examples of both approaches; the Linen & Lace Café Curtains (see Chapter Four) uses the (nearly) invisible join and the Mixed-Warp Pillow Cover and the Tweed and Twill Pillow Cover (see Chapter Six) use a decorative seam. Or, skip the seam all together and use doubleweave to create seamless throws and pillows!

HOW TO: RUNNING STITCH

1   Cut your finishing yarn 3 times the length of your seam. This allows for the over/under movement of the yarn and tails for finishing.

2   Line up your fabric edges—these could be fringed or hemmed fabric—and pin. Leaving a 6" (15.2 cm) tail and using a tapestry needle threaded with your finishing yarn, weave with the needle (this is called "needleweaving") under your chosen number of warp yarns following 1 weft pick (Figure 1). You can make the stitches as large or as small as you desire. The larger the stitch, the more it will show, but the less stable the seam.

3   Secure the ends by knotting the yarn around 1 warp or weft thread and bury it in the interior of the fabric. Pull it away from the surface 3" (7.5 cm) away from the knot, then trim flush to the surface. Do the same with the starting tail.

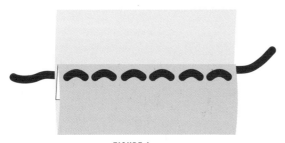

FIGURE 1

HOW TO: INVISIBLE SEAM

1   Place 2 panels of fabric next to each other so that the weft yarns line up and the same side is facing up—front or back, it doesn't matter which.

2   Cut a matching yarn 4 times the length of the fabric to allow for take-up.

3   Working on the inside of the selvedge thread, insert the needle from the back of the cloth on top of the first pick of 1 panel—in this case, working from right to left—and then under the same corresponding pick on the other side.

    Pull the yarn through and, working on the same left panel, insert it through the top of the fabric and top of the next weft thread, then insert it from the back side of the corresponding weft thread on the other, right panel.

4   Work another stitch from the top of the right panel and under the corresponding pick on the left panel (Figure 2).

5   Continue in this manner, snugging the seam as you go without over tightening it. If your fabric is slightly irregular, skip 1 or 2 wefts to keep the fabric from skewing or puckering at the seam.

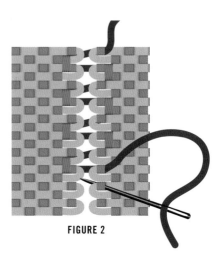

FIGURE 2

HOW TO: ESKIMO JOIN

1   Fold your fabric in half or lay 2 pieces on top of one another so the top and bottom edges line up.

2   Using yarn 3 times the length of your seam and a tapestry needle, create a base line of running stitches. Start at your desired number of threads from the edge and sew the 2 layers of cloth together using the running stitch and traveling over and under 2 warp ends or weft picks, depending on where your seams lay on the fabric (Figure 3).

3   Cut another length of yarn 5 times the length of your fabric. Position the fabric so that the seam is facing you. The top of the stitch is the edge of the running stitch that is farthest away from you; the bottom is the side that is closest (Figure 3).

4   Starting at the back of the fabric, work your second row of stitches from right to left. Pass your needle from top to bottom of the second running stitch. Bring the needle up and around to the top layer and pass it under the first stitch from the bottom to the top.

   Pass the needle through from top to bottom of the next running stitch on the top layer and around and through the same stitch on the back (which you already worked) from bottom to top.

   Bring the needle back around and work through the same stitch on the top, which has already been worked.

5   Continue working in this manner until all of the running stitches have been worked. You will have 2 ends running through every stitch.

6   Needleweave in the ends, looping through the stitches on the back that have only 1 stitch running through them.

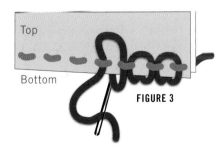

Top

Bottom

FIGURE 3

Off-Loom Fringe Finishes

SETUP

1   If you plan to work your fringe off the loom, weave headers on both ends (see Chapter Two) with scrap yarn to keep the weft in place until you are ready to work your fringe treatment.

2   Remove the work from the loom and place it on a flat surface. You may need to place a weight on the cloth to keep it from moving about and to give you tension to work against.

3   Using embroidery scissors, carefully cut the header in half. If your warp is relatively narrow, remove half of the scrap yarn. If it is wider, you may want to cut the header out in shorter chunks.

4   Work the finishing, whatever it may be, in that section. Cut away the second half of the header, working that section. Repeat this process until you have completed tying your fringe.

5   If you are working 2 rows of knots, work the first one all the way across the warp, then go back and work the second row.

HOW TO: OVERHAND KNOT

1   Working from the outside in, tie overhand knots loosely by forming a loop with the fringe and then slipping the tail through the center of that loop (Figures 4 and 5).

2   Snug the knot loosely up against the base of the cloth.

3   After you have tied all the knots, go back and tighten them, adjusting as necessary so they line up neatly.

FIGURE 4

FIGURE 5

HOW TO: STAGGERED KNOTS

1 Working from the outside in, tie overhand knots loosely, snugging them up to the edge of the weaving.

2 After you have tied all of the knots, go back and tighten them, adjusting as necessary so they line up neatly.

3 Work another row of overhand knots, offset from the first, by taking half of 1 knotted group and tying it to half of its neighbor (Figure 6) .

3 Pull on both ends to tighten. Trim the tails flush with the wrap. If desired, put a dot of liquid seam sealer such Fray Check to further secure the area where you trimmed the tails (Figure 10).

4 Work the rest of the warp groupings in this same- manner. Then work another row of bound warps, offsetting them from the first by binding together half of the warp ends from the first group and half of the warp ends from the second group.

5 Continue working staggered rows as long as de- sired.

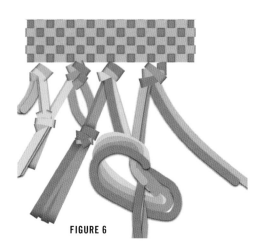

FIGURE 6

FIGURE 7

FIGURE 8

HOW TO: STAGGERED BOUND WARP

1 Use a fine cotton or silk thread to bind the warp ends together in decorative bundles.

   Cut a length of fine yarn 12" (30.5 cm) long. Make a loop with the yarn and place it on the chosen group of warp threads so that the loop is at the bottom, 1 end of the yarn is at the top and the other is your working end (Figure 7). Wrap the yarn around your chosen number of warp ends and itself 5–8 times, being careful to cover the front and back equally (Figure 8).

2 Thread the working end of the yarn through a tapestry needle and run it through the (Figure 9).

FIGURE 9

FIGURE 10

HOW TO: STAGGERED MACRAMÉ SQUARE KNOTS

NOTE: *Each individual knot is worked over 4 ends or groupings. The entire finish is worked over 2 rows.*

1 To work the first half of the knot, pass the leftmost end over the 2 adjacent ends to its right and under the rightmost yarn (Figure 11).

   Pass the rightmost yarn behind the 2 adjacent ends to its left and through the loop formed by the leftmost thread (Figure 12).

2 To work the second half of the knot, work the same arrangement in the opposite direction, first passing the rightmost end over the 2 adjacent ends to its left and under the leftmost yarn (Figure 13). Then pass the leftmost yarn behind the 2 adjacent ends to its right and through the loop formed by the rightmost thread (Figure 14).

3 Snug the knot.

4 Work the next 4 threads in the same manner, adjusting so that the new knot is even with the knot to its left. Continue working until you have worked all of the warp ends.

5 Work a second row of knots, staggering them from the first row by using the first 2 ends from the first knot and the second 2 ends from their neighbor to the left (Figure 15).

6 You will have free-hanging ends on either side of the ends encased in the knot. Tie the free-hanging ends together, starting with the first free-hanging end of the right side of the first knot and tying it to the free-hanging end of the second knot (Figure 16).

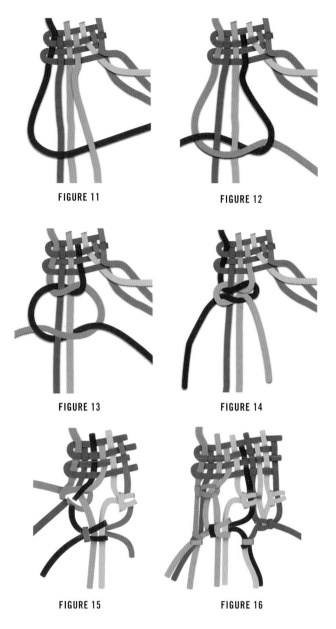

FIGURE 11   FIGURE 12

FIGURE 13   FIGURE 14

FIGURE 15   FIGURE 16

HOW TO: 4-STRANDED FLAT BRAID

NOTE: *Work this braid over 4 ends.*

1   Divide a group of 4 ends in half (Figure 17). Bring the outside left end over the inside left strand.

2   Bring the outside right end under the inside right end and over what is now the left inside end (from Step 1). The ends that were on the outside are now on the inside (Figure 18).

3   Continuing working to desired length (Figure 19), then secure with an overhand knot.

HOW TO: WOVEN EDGE

NOTE: *This is a clean finish that leaves 1 small braid at 2 corners of the work.*

1   Starting on the left side of the work, tension 4 ends with your left hand. Weave a closed pair of tweezers in and out of these 4 ends, traveling under/over/under to create a small shed (Figure 20).

2   Grab the fourth warp end with the tweezers and pull it through the shed. Pull the thread taut to straighten and then, directing it upward, lay it on the fabric out of the way of the other ends (Figures 21 and 22).

3   Add the warp end to the right of the 3 remaining ends and work Steps 1 and 2 again. Continue working in this manner until you have worked your way across the end of the fabric.

4   You will have 4 ends left at 1 edge of the fabric. Work a short 4-stranded braid to finish off.

5   Using an embroidery needle, bury each end into the warp path of its neighbor to the right for ½" (1.3 cm), then trim flush with the fabric.

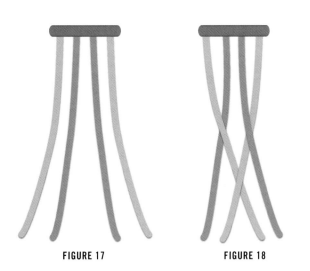

FIGURE 17   FIGURE 18

FIGURE 19

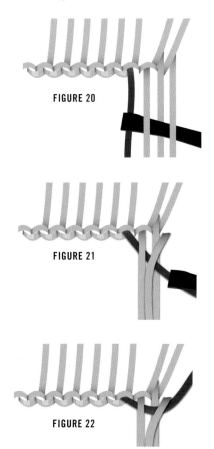

FIGURE 20

FIGURE 21

FIGURE 22

On-Loom Fringe Finishes

An alternative to knotting is to secure your weft in place while the work is still on the loom. Using a stitch, such as hemstitch or embroidery stitch, creates a nice, clean finish. When the cloth comes off the loom, nothing further is necessary before you wash your project. After washing, trim the fringe to your desired length using a rotary cutter and self-healing mat.

HOW TO: HEMSTITCH

Hemstitching is the most common on-loom stitch. It creates a secure finish with an open fringe.

1 Begin your project, leaving a tail of weft yarn 6 times the width of your project.

2 Weave 1" (2.5 cm), then thread the tail through a tapestry needle.

3 Decide on the number of warp and weft ends you want to work into each bundle, such as 2 warp ends and 2 weft picks (Figures 23 and 24). They don't have to be the same number.

4 Secure the edge by wrapping the selvedge thread twice with the needle and working yarn.

5 Insert your needle on top of the desired number of weft picks, such as 2. Exit the needle at an angle under your desired number of weft picks and warp ends. This forms a vertical stitch on the front and an angled stitch on the back (Figure 23).

Pull the needle and thread through, then encase the 2 warp ends behind the working thread (Figure 24).

6 Keep working the stitches until you have reached the edge of the cloth.

7 Needleweave the tail back into the cloth 1" (2.5 cm) and trim the working yarn to 2" (5 cm).

8 Wash the fabric, then trim the tail flush to the cloth.

The wrong side of the work will have angled stitches, and the right side will have straight stitches.

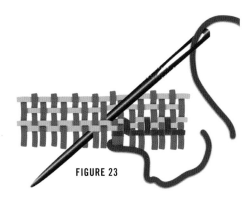

FIGURE 23

FIGURE 24

HOW TO: EMBROIDERY STITCH

Embroidery stitch, also called chain stitch, works up faster than hemstitching, but it is less secure. It is a good choice for fringe that is 1" (2.5 cm) or longer or to quickly staystitch an edge for hand hemming.

1 To work the stitch, form an open-tensioned loop with the working yarn and place the needle under your desired number of ends, such as 2 (Figure 25).

2 Thread the needle through the bottom curve of the loop (Figure 26). Pull the loop tight.

3 Continue working in this manner across the warp, keeping the yarn under moderate tension at all times.

HOW TO: CLOVE-HITCH KNOT EDGING

1 Cut a 2½ yd (2.3 m) length of the finishing yarn— smooth cotton works best. Thread it through a tapestry needle.

2 Leaving a 6" (15.2 cm) tail and working from left to right, wrap the yarn around the desired number of warp ends   in a figure-eight style, threading the yarn over the upper loop and under the lower loop (Figure 27).

Press the knot so that it is touching the woven picks and cinch tight.

4 Continue working the knots across the width of the warp, being careful to maintain a straight line as you work and not push the weft picks so they become compressed (Figure 28).

5 Needleweave both tails 1" (2.5 cm) into the cloth.

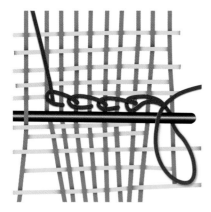

FIGURE 25

FIGURE 27

FIGURE 28

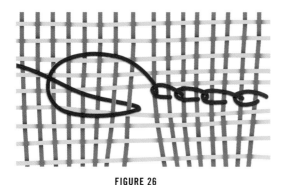

FIGURE 26

HOW TO: USING A ROTARY CUTTER

It is difficult to cut a straight edge along the fringe with a pair of scissors. I prefer to trim my fringe with a rotary cutter and a self-healing mat, which are common tools of the quilter.

1   Lay your work on the mat, lining up the edge of the cloth with one of the straight guide marks on the mat.

2   Rake your fringe so it lays flat. Then, following the appropriate guide line, trim the fringe with the rotary cutter.

Laundering Your Handwovens

Most woven cloth should be wet-finished to fully settle into itself. There are a few exceptions in this book such as the Hemp Hot Pads (see Chapter Five), the Fabric Stash Rag Rug (see Chapter Four), and the Two-Color Krokbragd Rug (see Chapter Seven). The material used in these projects don't bloom, or expand, when washed, and therefore don't need to be wet-finished to reveal their true beauty.

If your fabric seems less than perfect when you remove it from the loom, it, as the saying goes, will all come out in the wash.

Yarn manufacturers put the most conservative washing instruction on their yarn labels—comparable to food expiration dates, they allow you to have the best possible experience with the product, but they don't give you the full story. Most labels will instruct you to handwash. I have found that many yarns will hold up to machine washing on the gentle cycle, even benefiting from it. But you do need to pay very close attention to the fringe. Singles, softlyplied, many-plied, or blended yarn tends to fray. The only way to know for sure how a new yarn will finish is to sample.

HANDWASHING

Most accessories and textiles made from luxury fibers such as silk or cashmere should be washed by hand. Soak the fabric in lukewarm water with either a mild

or no-rinse detergent for 20 minutes. For household objects that are long and flat, I often do this in the bathtub where I can lay the whole project out. Rinse gently if necessary. Roll the project in a towel and press to remove excess water, taking care not to wring it. Dry the project flat on a clean towel. Trim the fringe to the desired length.

MACHINE WASHING

The secret to machine washing is to know your own washing machine—not all are created equal.

General instructions for machine washing on the gentle cycle are as follows: Machine wash on gentle with mild detergent. Add fabric softener if the fabric doesn't need to be scoured but softened. Either lay flat to dry on a clean towel or air-dry on low. Trim the fringe to the desired length.

I use the regular cycle for most kitchen and table items as well as projects made with linen or hemp that benefit from a rougher finish. Machine wash on regular with a mild detergent. Tumble dry on low. Press immediately if necessary. Linens, such as the Fresh Baked Bread Cloth (see Chapter Four) benefits from a good hot press while the fabric is still a bit damp—it will bring out the shine. Trim the fringe to the desired length.

SPOT CLEANING

You can spot clean any spills by allowing the fabric to soak for a while in warm water and then very gently rubbing the area with a clean cloth.

If the stain is greasy, dampen the cloth and then sprinkle the spot with cornstarch. Allow it to rest for a day and then either blot with a damp towel or, if the fabric will hold up (think rugs), use a soft bristle brush to scrub the area. Rinse clean. This method works best on colorfast yarn. If you are using hand-dyed or other yarns you fear may run, test first.

There is a special satisfaction in creating a textile for your home—finding a pattern, selecting the yarn, setting up the loom, weaving the cloth, and finding the perfect finish. Trimming that last bit of fringe for the big reveal is a satisfying moment. It's a good time to pause and give yourself a pat on the back. Well-done, you.

Glossary

ADVANCE THE WARP: To release tension on the cloth and wind the woven cloth onto the front beam, then re-tension the warp to continue weaving.

BALANCED PLAIN WEAVE: A fabric in which there is the same number of warp ends and weft picks per 1" (2.5 cm).

BEAT: To bring the rigid heddle to the fell of the cloth to align and pack the weft.

BEATER: A device used to position each weft pick. This is the same as the rigid heddle on a rigid-heddle loom.

BOAT SHUTTLE: A shuttle with a spinning bobbin.

COUNT SYSTEM: A yarn classification system based on the number of yards in a pound of a standard size.

DRESSING THE LOOM: To measure the warp and wind it on the loom.

END (WARP END): One thread or multiple threads that act as one in the warp.

ENDS PER INCH (EPI): The number of warp threads in 1" (2.5 cm).

FELL: The part of the cloth where the weaving action occurs. It is also the last laid pick.

FLOAT: Yarn where a weft pick or warp end doesn't travel in the normal over/under/over path.

FRINGE: The unwoven warp that is intentionally left at the ends of woven cloth.

GRIST: The size of a yarn.

HAND: The way the cloth feels.

HEADER: The first 1"–2" (2.5–5 cm) of weaving (usually done with scrap yarn) to spread out the warp ends to their full weaving width.

HEDDLES: The molded plastic pieces in the rigid heddle through which the warp ends are threaded.

HEMSTITCHING: A way to secure the first and last weft picks of cloth.

INTERSTITIAL FRINGE: Unwoven warp between the multiple items that will become fringe in the final project.

LEADER YARN: An inelastic contrasting yarn that marks the desired path to follow when measuring the warp on a warping board.

LOOM WASTE: The amount of extra warp left over after weaving.

PICK (OR SHOT): One pass of the shuttle through the shed.

PICKS PER INCH (PPI): The number of weft picks in 1" (2.5 cm) of woven cloth.

PICK-UP STICK: A flat stick with at least one beveled point used to pick up individual warp ends.

PLAIN WEAVE: Cloth woven so that one weft pick travels over/under one warp.

PLIED YARN: Yarn made up of two or more singles yarn.

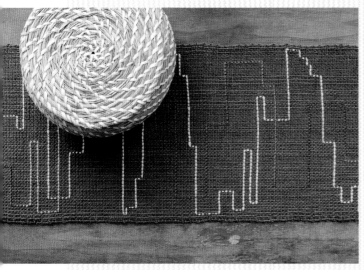

RIGID HEDDLE: Device that determines the spacing of the warp and acts as the beater.

SELVEDGES: The edges of the cloth where the weft exits one shed and enters the next.

SETT: The spacing of the warp ends in the heddle; see ends per inch (EPI).

SHED: The open space that is created when the heddle is lifted up or down.

SHED BLOCKS: Devices used to hold the rigid heddle in the up or down position to produce a shed.

SHOT: See pick.

SHUTTLE: Device used to pass the weft yarn back and forth across the warp as you weave.

SINGLES: A single strand of spun fiber.

STICK SHUTTLE: A shuttle typically used when weaving on rigid-heddle looms.

TAKE-UP: The extra amount of yarn needed to allow for the weft to bend over and under the warp threads.

THREADS: Term used interchangeably with "yarn" to describe the warp or weft.

THROW: To pass the shuttle into the shed.

WARP: Threads held taut on a loom. It is also the act of dressing the loom.

WARP DOMINANT: Cloth in which the warp yarn ends completely cover the weft picks.

WARP-EMPHASIS WEAVE: Cloth in which there are more warp ends per 1" (2.5 cm) than weft picks.

WARP END: An individual warp yarn or thread.

WARPING BOARD: Device used to easily measure the warp ends in preparation for threading the loom.

WARPING PEG: Used to hold and measure the warp during the direct warping method.

WARPING STICK: Thin flat stick used to separate the warp while winding it onto the warp beam.

WEAVE: The process of crossing taut warp threads with a weft thread.

WEAVE STRUCTURE: The pattern of interlacements that are created by either the loom setup or the warp manipulation of the weaver.

WEAVER'S CROSS: A part of the warp formed when winding yarn on a warping board. It keeps the warp threads in order and minimizes tangles when the weaver threads the loom.

Resources

OTHER BOOKS AND VIDEOS BY LIZ GIPSON FROM INTERWEAVE:

Weaving Made Easy

Video Workshops:

Life After Warping: Weaving Well on Your Rigid-Heddle Loom

Slots and Holes: 3 Ways to Warp a Rigid-Heddle Loom

Twice as Nice: Weaving With Two Heddles on a Rigid-Heddle Loom

Double Your Fun: Double weave on a RigidHeddle Loom

BOOKS

Hands on Rigid Heddle Weaving by Betty Davenport (Interweave)

Inventive Weaving on a Little Loom: Discover the Full Potential of the Rigid-Heddle Loom, for Beginners and Beyond by Syne Mitchell (Storey Publishing)

Textures and Patterns for the Rigid Heddle Loom by Betty Linn Davenport (self-published)

The Complete Book of Drafting for Handweavers by Madelyn van der Hoogt (Shuttle Craft Books)

The Weaver's Idea Book: Creative Cloth on a Rigid Heddle Loom by Jane Patrick (Interweave)

Woven Treasures by Sara Lamb (Interweave)

The Xenakis Technique for the Construction of Four Harness Textiles by Athanosios David Xenakis (Golden Fleece Publications)

Interweave's Compendium of Finishing Techniques by Naomi McEneely (Interweave)

YARN AND TOOL SUPPLIERS

These fine companies generously offered support for the making of this book:

BERROCO
berroco.com

BROWN SHEEP COMPANY
brownsheep.com

CASCADE YARNS
cascadeyarns.com

CRYSTAL PALACE YARNS
straw.com

COTTON CLOUDS
cottonclouds.com

CLASSIC ELITE YARNS
classiceliteyarns.com

BE SWEET
besweetproducts.com

DARN GOOD YARN
darngoodyarn.com

FANCY TIGER CRAFTS
fancytigercrafts.com

HALYCON YARN
halcyonyarn.com

KNITTING FERVER
knittingfever.com

LION BRAND
lionbrand.com

LOUET NORTH AMERICA
louet.com

LUNATIC FRINGE
lunaticfringeyarns.com

PRISM YARN
prismayarn.com

ROWAN YARNS
knitrowan.com

SCHACHT SPINDLE COMPANY
schachtspindle.com

Acknowledgments

Weaving twenty-one projects and writing an accompanying manuscript in fifteen months is a monumental task—a fun, challenging, life-affirming, soul-searching act of will. Good manuscripts come together with the help of many individuals beside the author. Support from family and friends is critical, and I'm grateful to have the support of both.

In particular, my husband, Kip, who thinks that playing with yarn is cool; my mother, Martha, who believes that a great and enduring dedication to your craft is a perfectly fine way to lead your life; and my father, David, who showed me that that making stuff brings a kind of satisfaction that can't be found in a box.

The keen eyes of editors make books possible—Kerry, Lisa, Michelle, Leslie, Susan, Karla, and Nancy made these pages much better than I would have alone.

To the countless yarn suppliers and the tool makers that have supported me and weavers like me throughout the years, thank you. The know-how I have gathered throughout the years is because others have championed this loom and the yarn life before me, and my students who constantly inspire me to do better.

I am eternally grateful for the opportunity to be a working weaver, and I am constantly reminded, through you, the reading weaver, of the sheer joy of hanging out on the warped side of yarn.

ABOUT THE AUTHOR

Liz Gipson enjoys living a yarn-filled life. She hosts a popular website, Yarnworker.com, a source for rigid-heddle know-how and inspiration. As the author of the newly revised and updated *Weaving Made Easy* and host of four instructional videos on rigid-heddle weaving produced by Interweave, Liz delights in helping weavers find ease in their weaving. She writes about weaving and the yarn life for many popular fiber-related magazines, websites, and blogs, and she teaches workshops throughout the country.

METRIC CONVERSION

TO CONVERT	TO	MULTIPLY BY
Inches	Centimeters	2.54
Centimeters	Inches	0.4
Feet	Centimeters	30.5
Centimeters	Feet	0.03
Yards	Meters	0.9
Meters	Yards	1.1

Index

A

abrasion, yarn 15
acrylic 13

B

bast fibers 12
beat 162
beater 162; tapestry 23
boat shuttle 162; winding 26

C

cartoon, making 91
cellulose fibers 9–10
clasped weft 162
charts, following 32–33
colors, choosing 79; joining yarn 25
composition, weaving 79
cottolin 12
cotton 9; craft 11; crochet 10–11;
    mercerized 10; naturally colored 10;
    novelty 11; organic 10; recycled 11
cotton carpet warp 10
count system 14–15; 162
curtain hanging options 59

D

direct warping 138–141
doubled ends, winding 26
doubleweave 118–119
drafts, reading 74
drawdown 74
dressing the loom 162

E

embroidery stitch 159
ends 162; number of 32
ends per inch (epi)
equipment 32
eskimo join 155

F

fabric for weft 44–45
fabric removal from loom 152
fell 162
fibers, bast 12; cellulose 9–10;
    synthetic
Fibonacci sequence 79
fine warps 149
finishing 152–153
floats 162; fixing 152
4-stranded flat braid 158
fringes 16, 155–160, 162; interstitial
    162

G

Golden Mean 79
grist 162
guide, paper 22

H

hand 162
handwashing handwovens 161
header 162; weaving a 20
heddle rod 29
heddles 5, 162
hemming 152–153
hemp 12
hemstitch 159, 162
holes and slots 21

I

indirect warping 138, 143–145
interstitial fringe 162

J

cjoining yarn colors 25
jute 12

K

knots, cloth-hitch 160; macramé
    square 157; overhand 155;
    staggered 154; staggered bound
    warp 154
krokbragd pattern 135

L

leader yarn 143–145, 162
linen 12, 53
log cabin pattern 107
long warps 148–149
loom waste 162

M

machine-washing handwovens 161
measuring cloth 22
mercerized cotton 10
metric conversion chart 165
mistakes, fixing 26
multiple projects on loom 22

N

notions 32
nylon 13

O

off-loom fringe finishes 155–158
on-loom fringe finishes 159–160

P

packing warp 149
pick 162
picks per inch (ppi) 32, 162
pick-up sticks 27–28, 162
pinch-and-pull yarn test 15
plain weave 162, balanced 162
ply 8–9, 162
ply-splitting yarns 24
prickle factor 13
put-up 14

R

rayon 13
rigid-heddle loom, what is a 5, 163
rotary cutter, using 160
running stitch 154

S

seam, invisible 154
seams, joining 154–155
selvedges 20–21, 27, 163; weights for 21
sett 32, 163
shed 163
shed blocks 163
shot see pick
shuttles 163, winding boat 26
silk, artificial see rayon
singles yarn 8, 163
size, finished 32
slots and holes 21
Soysilk 13
spot-cleaning handwovens 161
stick shuttle 163
structure, weave 32
superwash yarns
synthetic fibers 13

T

tails, tucking 24
take-up 163
tapestry beater 23
temple, using a 22
Tencel 13
threads 163
throw 163
traveling weft 24
twill /3, 100
2-heddle threading 146–147
2-heddle warping 138–141
2-heddles and 4 shafts 147

W

warp 15, 163; advancing 20–21, 162; packing 149
warp color order charts 33
warp dominant 163
warp-emphasis weave 163
warp end 162, 163
warp length 32
warping board 143–144, 163
warping cross 143–145, 163
warping guide for wide, long and fine warps 148–149
warping peg 138–139, 163
warping stick 163
warping recommendation 32
warping techniques 138
weave 163
weave structure 32, 163
weaver's cross 143–145, 163
weaving instructions, reading 32 33
weaving vs knitting yarns 14
weaving width 32
weft 15; clasped 162
weft color order charts 33
weft yarns, managing multiple 23–25; ply-splitting 24; traveling 24; tucking 24
weft angle 20
wide warps 148
wool yarns 12–13
woolen spun 9
worsted spun 9
woven edge fringe 158

Y

yarn for weaving 9, see also threads
yarn material, raw 8
yarn, choosing 15; singles 8; superwash 13; weaving vs knitting 14; wool 12–13
yarns 32
yarn test, abrasion 15; pinch-and-pull 15

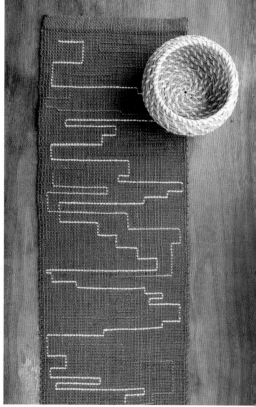